BURST!

Busting Old Patterns, Creating New Possibilities

Hillary —
Burst into winning ways!
Carol W

A "Guide and Apply" Book for Life

SHERRY M. WINN, DIANE CHEW, VIRGINIA SUE TARLTON

BURST!

Busting Old Patterns, Creating New Possibilities

A "Guide and Apply" Book for Life

© 2017 Sherry M. Winn, Diane Chew, Virginia Sue Tarlton

International Standard Book Number (ISBN): 978-1542383585

Printed in the United States of America

Contents

Relationships

Emotions

Introduction

Are you at a point in life where you feel stuck in frustrating patterns leading to the same old results with your health, wealth, relationships or emotions?

Are you ready for a burst of creativity, inspiration and joy?

If so, you've come to the right place!

We all develop patterns at an early age to help us navigate through the uncharted waters of life and some have served us well. But many patterns are conditioned reflexes that get triggered when we're upset, and seem to have a life of their own. They suck us down like quicksand and block our access to fresh perspectives and new possibilities.

We can tell when we're stuck in old patterns by the nature of the questions we're asking — questions that come from a fearful mindset that doesn't know what to do.

Questions such as:

- Am I ever going to get ahead financially?
- Why is this relationship so hard?
- How do I let go of the past?

We usually try to answer these questions from our own point of view and singular experience — experience that is derived from our own patterns. But then we wonder why it's so hard to get different results.

We know. We've been there. And we're here to help.

This compilation of wisdom is the result of our own search for answers to a different question: "How do we bust out of our old patterns and create new possibilities?"

But unlike many self help approaches that offer "answers" and promises for problem resolution, we're offering a set of principles and perspectives, and a process for taking inspired action:

- 7 Wisdom Principles that you can apply to ANY situation,

- Multiple perspectives on *how* to apply those principles, and

- Application questions so you can design a solution that helps to bust your old patterns and open up the doors for a burst of new possibilities.

This is not a quick fix for your life, but it is a *lasting* one. When you live your life by a set of principles rather than scrambling frantically for answers to every challenge life throws at you, you develop a sense of trust in yourself and your own ability to handle whatever comes your way. And with that comes peace of mind, more priceless than gold.

The 7 Wisdom Principles included in this book were derived from the combined decades of our lives — decades of searching and studying and applying what we learned over and over until we proved the principles to ourselves. They work. Period. Every time… if you're willing to embrace the following values:

1. Value of Commitment — Are you ready for a change or do you just want to complain? Are you settling for just "trying" to change or are you willing to make a commitment to yourself for that change to happen?

2. Value of Consistency — Are you willing to apply the principles long enough to bust your patterns and create new possibilities? Are you willing to trust the process and have patience with yourself and others?

3. Value of Compassion — Are you willing to release self-judgment and the energies of blame and shame and cultivate a sense of tenderness toward your suffering without buying into it? Are you willing to have compassion for your conditioning and expand into possibilities that you've only dared to dream about up until now?

If you're willing to say "yes" to those questions — if you're even *willing to be willing* to say "yes" to each one, then you're ready to live your life by design — YOUR design — rather than default.

Allow us to be your guides as you bust your old patterns and open up to a new way of thinking about yourself and your health, wealth, relationships and emotions — the facets of life that take up the majority of our time and attention. Even though we are all spiritual beings, we are all having a human experience. We share the most fundamental needs to survive and desires to thrive. So there's no need to try to go it alone. We connected with each other in answer to our own hearts crying out for help and this book is our joint offering to connect with you.

Life doesn't have to feel so hard and you don't have to be stuck with old patterns of thinking and reacting. There IS an easier way, and the 7 Wisdom Principles illuminate the path so you don't have to keep bumping around in the dark. As you consider the questions that relate to the most pressing issues you face at the moment, consider our perspectives with a spirit of curiosity to discern what you can learn from our experience. Ask yourself how it can help you to bust through old patterns and create new possibilities. You know more than you think you do, and once you realize that, you can relax into the flow of life with more ease and grace and joy.

Are you ready for your *BURST!* of creativity, inspiration and joy?

Let's begin!

With love,

Sherry, Diane and Sue

Options for How to Use This Book

Remember all the times you've detoured from your path by replacing new programs with even newer ones? When you embrace The 7 Wisdom Principles and apply them with commitment, consistency and compassion, you will stay on the path you are designing, no matter how many program shifts you make.

This "guide and apply" book allows you to explore and expand options to your thinking.

For commitment, keep the principles handy and refer to them often.

For consistency, continually ask yourself what principle you are currently using and how it applies to what you're experiencing.

For compassion, practice observing your thinking and your behaviors without judgment. Consider adding new people and experiences to your life to celebrate you on your journey and encourage you on your path.

We designed this book to be flexible and to support you as you explore life's questions. To make the principles part of your daily life, we have a few suggestions about how to use this "guide and apply" book format.

1. Leave the book out in a handy place — by your bed, in the bathroom, on a coffee table. Pick the book up, flip to one of the questions and read the answers with an open and curious mind to see how they relate to a situation you or someone you care about is facing.

2. Work with one question at a time:

    a. Scan the Table of Contents and note the questions that are in alignment with the most pressing issues you have about your health, wealth, relationships or emotions.

    b. Consider which one would give you the most peace if you could come up with some new answers.

    c. Read the associated responses.

    d. Answer the chapter questions and decide on an approach that is totally within your own control.

    e. Apply that approach for thirty days. Observe your own experience objectively, without judgment, including how others are reacting to you. Note your observations in a journal or in this book.

    f. At the end of 30 days, assess your approach and your results. (A lot of us forget this step!)

    g. Congratulate yourself along the way for being willing to take control of your life and design it your way!

3. Work with one principle at a time:

    a. Read through the principles in the chapter entitled "The 7 Wisdom Principles" and pick one that resonates with you the most right now.

b. Read the principle every day and ask Spirit the question, "How can this principle help me to be in the flow of love and abundance today in all areas of my life?"

c. Work with the same principle for 30 days. Observe your own experience objectively, without judgment, including how others are reacting to you. Note your observations in a journal or in this guide and apply book.

d. At the end of 30 days, assess how the principle has impacted your results.

e. Congratulate yourself along the way for being willing to take control of your life and design it *your* way!

4. Partner up with a friend or study group to discuss different questions, how you applied the principles and the results you experienced. Ask for help, brainstorm solutions, share your successes.

5. Seek more personalized, targeted assistance by choosing to invest in your own coach. For most of us, it can be challenging to stay committed when we're attempting to make changes all by ourselves and we would do better partnering with someone with the training and tools to support our shift from the mental, physical and emotional patterns that no longer serve us. By gaining clarity on where to put our focus, regular check-in sessions to discuss our progress along the way, and consistent reminders to celebrate as we go, we can all experience what it truly means to "enjoy the journey" — NOW!

We are all certified coaches and it would be our pleasure and delight to hear from you and discuss whether personal coaching is appropriate for you at this time. We all offer long- and short-term programs to best address your needs. Please contact any or all of us to schedule an introductory conversation about where you are in your life right now and where you think you'd like to be. Just put "schedule coaching conversation" in the subject line, and let the healing begin!

Coach Sherry Winn (**coachwinn@coachwinnspeaks.com**)
Diane Chew (**diane@recoveryourbrilliance.com**)
Sue Tarlton (**sue@tappinginschools.com**)

The 7 Wisdom Principles

Benefits of using universal guiding principles:

* **Principles offer an easy and efficient approach to handling life's challenges and opportunities:** a small number of principles taken in different combinations covers an infinite variety of specific circumstances.

* **Principles provide for free will and creative expression:** they serve as a "guide" to help you, based on the way things work, versus "rules" you have to follow to please some higher authority. (And those "higher authority rules" are often broken, avoided or ignored, followed by the requisite guilt… never a peaceful solution.)

* **Principles save time and energy:** as you apply universal principles to different life situations, you come to trust that they work. When you encounter similar situations, you'll have increased ability to respond faster and more effectively.

1. **Principle of Connection:** *We are one with all that is.*

   Energy is the basic component and power of the Universe and cannot be created or destroyed, only transformed. Within that energy is an eternal, infinite intelligence: Source Energy (Infinite Intelligence, God, Love, Universal Spirit, Higher Power) to which we are all connected and therefore we are connected to one another. Our experience of feeling separated from our Source and from one another comes from guilt, judgment and blame. As we are willing to clear the barriers to the presence of Source Energy, which is unconditionally loving and supportive at all times, we experience our world and everything in it as safe, loving and generous. Through the removal of our own obstacles to the presence of love, we can claim and experience the power of being one with all that is.

2. **Principle of Focus:** *Our thoughts create our reality.*

   We are an extension of Source Energy in this physical reality and without any resistance, the flow of Source Energy is abundant and continuous. We can impact the flow of Source Energy through us by expanding or contracting ourselves through our thoughts, which create our beliefs and in turn create our reality. Choosing and practicing positive thoughts expands us and opens us up to the flow of Source Energy and abundance. Choosing to focus on negative thoughts contracts us and constricts the flow of Source Energy, creating limitations in our abilities, talents and potential and our circumstances overall.

3. **Principle of Now:** *Our point of power is in the present moment.*

   All that we have is the current moment: the past is gone and the future is not yet here. When we choose to focus on either the past or the future, we lose our point of power, which is now. As we accept what is happening in the present moment without resistance, we are able to change what is within our power to change and have the wisdom to accept what we cannot change without wasting mental or physical energy. As we let go of our resistance to what is and focus on what we appreciate about the present moment instead, we open ourselves up to the flow of Source Energy which is in infinite supply and available equally to everyone. Living in the present moment allows us to experience more grace, peace and joy.

4. **Principle of Unconditional Love:** *All love given returns.*

   We are completed through our ability to unconditionally love ourselves and others, accepting and owning all of who we are without judgment or expectations. Unconditional love requires the awareness that forgiveness has already happened. Nothing we or anybody else has done is held against us, and we are all worthy of unconditional love. The more we are willing to give love (peace, joy, compassion, understanding, etc.) to others, the more we transcend our own fears and open ourselves up to the flow of love and abundance in our lives. When we choose a path of hatred, deceit or pain, we experience the results of those actions. Likewise, when we choose gratitude, joy and service, those actions return to us in kind. The more we give, the more we receive, as all love given returns.

5. **Principle of the Highest Good:** *Enjoying the journey.*

   Everything we experience is part of our journey and can be used for our highest good if we are willing to let go of the meaning we attach to behaviors, events and circumstances. Even though we have been carefully taught to evaluate and judge virtually everything we experience as right/wrong, good/bad, happy/sad, etc., our judgments are based on our past experiences and we cannot know what something really means in the present moment. As we let go of the meaning that we attach to our experiences and adopt a spirit of curiosity, we open ourselves up to the possibilities for learning and spiritual growth. We can recognize that all which seems to occur "to" us, can be used "for" us, which greatly reduces our suffering and allows us to enjoy the journey.

6. **Principle of Trust:** *Focus on the "what," not the "how."*

   We live in an abundant universe and are born with everything required to live an abundant life since we all have the freedom to make choices of what we think about, and our thoughts create our reality. When we have faith in our ability to create, we can focus on **what** we want with love and compassion, focusing on "this, or something better." We can then trust our higher selves as Source Energy — as Infinite Intelligence — to handle the details in ways our rational minds cannot conceive. As we allow events to unfold naturally, without resistance, we can experience the seeds of our faith and the certainty that we are one with our Creator and therefore worthy of experiencing the flow of abundance.

7. **Principle of Perception:** *What we experience is what we believe.*

   We attract into our lives the people, events and circumstances that are a reflection of our inner world and the beliefs we hold. The traits which we admire in ourselves, we will recognize in others and those which we resist in others we can find in ourselves if we are willing to look. Everything we experience is an opportunity to learn and to show us some aspect of who we are. Every experience reflects back to us our present state of consciousness like a mirror. As we accept this reflection as the gift that it is, we can use it to examine the beliefs we hold and release those that no longer serve us.

HEALTH

Contents

1. How do I partner with my body to access its innate wisdom?

2. What role do emotions/limiting beliefs play in the manifestation and healing of disease?

3. How do I access the wisdom of my heart?

4. I've done so much spiritual work, why do I still have so many physical problems/challenges?

5. How do I let go of my anxiety and/or depression?

6. How do we explain physical pain to ourselves?

1

How do I partner with my body to access its innate wisdom?

ANSWERS:

——————— By Sherry ———————

Do you think of your body as muscle, tissue and organs or do you think of your body as consciousness speaking to you?

Your body can converse with you if you will take the time to listen.

Our physical bodies have a conscious energy system or body wisdom which tells us if we are headed in the wrong direction. The body conveys messages to us in the form of symptoms which we describe as pain or disease.

If you take time to intimately know your body and to feel your emotions, you will understand the messages your body sends to you.

What we tend to do is to resist, ignore, or deny the messages being sent our way. Our body tells us we are in resistance by giving us clues to take action. (Principle of Focus/Now) These clues might be headaches, a tightening around our hearts, or a tear caught in our throats.

How many times have you ignored a gut feeling only to discover your gut was telling you that you needed to take action now?

As a basketball coach, I valued my body's instincts. My body intuitively shifted to alert me to switch defenses, substitute a player or call a timeout. While I heeded my body's instincts on the court, I refused to listen to my body's instructions off the court.

Off the court I believed if I shut off my instincts, then the emotional pain of abandonment, betrayal or fear would simply go away.

My body, knowing I needed to heal the emotion, kept my negative emotions stuffed inside its cells.

Our body is the vehicle to learn forgiveness and in learning forgiveness, learn how to love. (Principle of Unconditional Love) This is our journey — to heal ourselves.

────── By Diane ──────

To me, accessing the innate wisdom of the body is another way of accessing the wisdom of our higher self or Source. The Principle of Connection (#1) states that we are one with all that is, so therefore our minds, bodies and spirits are "One with the One." If we consistently invest in false beliefs, some version of "I'm to blame, they're wrong, I'm not good enough, things should be different," we'll feel it first as a negative emotion. If left unchecked, it will eventually show up as some form of "dis-ease" that can range from headaches to back pain to more serious disorders. So our bodies serve as spiritual alarm clocks, waking us up to the opportunity to partner up and get at the root source of what's really bothering us.

Suggestions for partnering up:

1. Practice self care by nourishing your body with good food, water and consistent movement. It's hard to hear the voice of your higher self when your body is deprived of what it needs to run efficiently.

2. Write a letter of appreciation to your body and then ask what it would like to say to you. Just start writing and see what comes out on the page.

3. Practice deep breathing on a regular basis. Inspiration can be defined as being "in Spirit" and also "to inhale." As we breathe in, we're literally breathing in Spirit. Try taking 10 slow, deep breaths to clear your chattering mind and access your higher wisdom.

4. Play with the experience of "non-doing:" meditation, prayer, walking in nature, lying on the ground, hugging a tree, etc. It's hard to access the wisdom of our bodies when we're so focused on getting things done. The more willing we are to create space in our minds by just *being* in the present moment, the easier it will be to access our body's loving messages.

By Sue

First, let's ask, "What sort of innate wisdom does the body have?" Let's use Principle 1 for this discussion — "We are one with all that is."

We need to make an assumption. If the body has wisdom available for access, and the body is one with all that is, then we can assume the body is one with wisdom of all kinds. From that, we can assume that the body knows whatever it is we want to know. Now, the title question makes sense.

You've seen people use a pendulum, read palms, take an x-ray, view MRI results and do all sorts of testing and observation to ask the body questions. Once a question is asked and answered, though, do we think that's a partnership? Not unless we act on that wisdom we gathered. We build that partnership over time, through trust. Your body needs to know it is "safe" to talk with you.

Create a safe space. Sit in a comfortable place. What's your talent? Do you write or draw or make objects? Maybe you doodle or create computer art. Perhaps you mold clay or create precision frames. No matter. Ask your body a question and then do what you do. Your body can guide your hands on your path. Allow the answer to emerge from your very essence and your very core. Don't think. Do.

Notice metaphors. Notice the songs that come to mind. Notice smells and sounds. Notice pictures that come to mind. These are clues. Compile the clues and notice the wisdom that poured forth. Like a dream, some symbols may appear that aren't clear to you. Simply and respectfully ask for others. At the end of this very sacred time, thank your body for its wisdom. You've learned a lot!

—————— By You ——————

1. What's the situation you'd like to change? (Just the facts, please!)

   _____

   _____

   _____

2. What opinions, thoughts, feelings do you have about the situation as it is now?

   a. Opinions:

      _____

      _____

      _____

b. Thoughts:

_____

_____

_____

c. Feelings:

_____

_____

_____

3. What results would you prefer? How would that make you feel?

_____

_____

_____

4. How does this compare with other situations you've wanted to change in the past?

_____

_____

_____

5. What patterns do you notice about your own reactions, behaviors and results on this topic?

_____

_____

_____

6. What limiting underlying belief(s) do you have about yourself or others, leading to this recurring pattern in your life?

   _____

   _____

   _____

   If you can't identify any limiting beliefs, consider the following:

   a. What opinion or judgment do you have about your situation?

      _____

      _____

      _____

   b. What do you keep telling yourself about your circumstances?

      _____

      _____

      _____

   c. When you think about your situation, what other pictures, persons, events or statements come to mind?

      _____

      _____

      _____

7. What principle(s) would most support you in busting your old pattern?

   _____

   _____

   _____

8. Are you willing to bust your pattern and experiment with a different approach in order to create new possibilities?

   ☐ Yes

   ☐ No

   ☐ Other

9. What bursts of inspiration have come to you about your situation after reading this section and answering these questions?

   _____

   _____

   _____

10. What 1-3 steps are you willing to take now in order to create new possibilities? (Note: Focus only on what's in your control.)

    _____

    _____

    _____

2

What role do emotions/ limiting beliefs play in the manifestation and healing of disease?

———— By Sherry ————

Dis-ease is created by us when we fail to align with thoughts of love.

Our negative thoughts are not original. They come from our parents, teachers, television, books and friends.

We are taught that guilt and shame are necessary to repent our "sins." This form of self-punishment creates more emotional pain. These emotional pain bodies attach themselves inside our cells.

To reverse the dis-ease you created, recognize the negative thoughts you feed yourself daily. When a thought comes up, rather than pushing the thought away, allow the thought to be felt. Allow the thought and the emotion with the thought to move through you. Be present with the thought. (Principle of Now)

A Course in Miracles states, "The miracle does nothing. All it does is undo. And thus it cancels out the interference to what has been done. It does not add but merely takes away." (page 589)

Your responsibility is to undo your negative thoughts and beliefs.

When you feel a negative thought move through you say, "I uncreate, destroy and cancel this thought and all emotions attached to this thought. I am an eternal being and creator. Since I created this thought. I can also release the thought. I align myself with love and God. I release all thoughts and attachments to the thoughts." (Principle of Unconditional Love)

Negative thoughts will reappear. Listen to your negative thoughts and allow them to move through you. (Principle of Now) When you resist thoughts they persist. By allowing negative thoughts to move through you, they have no power over you. (Principle of Focus)

The thought only holds the power you give it.

The key is the awareness of your thoughts and the consistency in releasing your thoughts rather than getting trapped in your story.

——————— By Diane ———————

This topic is near to my heart, literally and figuratively, since I almost went into congestive heart failure after unsuccessfully battling a disease for 12 years with mainstream medicine. Though traditional therapies helped me through the crisis, my symptoms — widespread and debilitating — didn't resolve until I did the deep work necessary to surface and surrender the limiting beliefs I held about myself. The childhood circumstances that laid the foundation for thinking I wasn't good enough, and the adult experiences that triggered them don't matter; they're just a story. What turned things around was getting clear on my false beliefs and partnering up with Spirit to heal them at the root source, moving towards a vision of wellness rather than trying to cure an illness.

The Principle of Unconditional Love (#4) states that "All love given returns." The more I was willing to love myself and my body just as I was without having to fix or change anything, the faster my body healed.

Our bodies don't create anything by themselves; they are for learning and communication. It's our thoughts that are creative according to The Principle of Focus (#2). The first thing in the world of form that gets impacted by our thoughts is our body. Whenever we experience a sense of "dis-ease," we're placing our faith in a false belief of separation instead of the truth stated in The Principle of Connection (#1) that "We are one with all that is."

Our false beliefs and the energy blockages they cause in our bodies can show up as anything from a general malaise to cancer. If we're willing to partner with our bodies and tune in to their messages, we can learn from their inherent wisdom — the higher part of ourselves that wants to come through and help us know the truth: that we are whole and complete just as we are.

By Sue

Tracking statements like "I have the weight of the world on my shoulders," "I can't see how we'll make it," "I can't stomach that any more," indicate that our folklore tied body issues to disease and distress.

Principle 2, "Our thoughts create our reality," says it all. What we focus on, we manifest. The more we include our bodies in our self-talk, the more our bodies create a home for the emotions that are being expressed. That's why I don't exactly understand people who swear by using body parts, body functions or body waste vocabulary in mean-spirited ways. Those body issues are important to our survival as humans and should be celebrated and thanked, not spoken of disparagingly. These people seem to have little respect for their humanity and I'd love to get some statistics about how many of them have physical problems related to the words they say in disgust.

Our bodies have taken on much more than they were intended to. Human bodies were designed to be "pass-through" mechanisms. We were to feel emotions and let them go. Some were so delicious, we started keeping them. Some hurt so much we decided we didn't want to feel the pain or re-live a specific incident ever again, so we suppressed them. Where do you think those hurts and even delicious feelings went? They had no place to go so they stayed in the body. Some depress our systems and some over-stimulate our systems. The imbalance created by this hoarding… consciously or subconsciously… from our genetic make-up and/or our past or current lives and/or emotions we picked up from others that don't even belong to us, all create imbalance and thus dis-ease in our bodies. Finding a way to clear all that is the trick to achieving good health.

—————— By You ——————

1. What's the situation you'd like to change? (Just the facts, please!)

    _____

    _____

    _____

2. What opinions, thoughts, feelings do you have about the situation as it is now?

    a. Opinions:

        _____

        _____

        _____

    b. Thoughts:

        _____

        _____

        _____

c. Feelings:

_____

_____

_____

3. What results would you prefer? How would that make you feel?

_____

_____

_____

4. How does this compare with other situations you've wanted to change in the past?

_____

_____

_____

5. What patterns do you notice about your own reactions, behaviors and results on this topic?

_____

_____

_____

6. What limiting underlying belief(s) do you have about yourself or others, leading to this recurring pattern in your life?

_____

_____

_____

If you can't identify any limiting beliefs, consider the following:

a. What opinion or judgment do you have about your situation?

_____

_____

_____

b. What do you keep telling yourself about your circumstances?

_____

_____

_____

c. When you think about your situation, what other pictures, persons, events or statements come to mind?

_____

_____

_____

7. What principle(s) would most support you in busting your old pattern?

_____

_____

_____

8. Are you willing to bust your pattern and experiment with a different approach in order to create new possibilities?

☐ Yes

☐ No

☐ Other

9. What bursts of inspiration have come to you about your situation after reading this section and answering these questions?

   _____

   _____

   _____

10. What 1-3 steps are you willing to take now in order to create new possibilities? (Note: Focus only on what's in your control.)

    _____

    _____

    _____

3

How do I access the wisdom of my heart?

———— By Sherry ————

How often have you heard people tell you to listen with your heart and not your head or vice versa? What is the difference between your heart and head and why would you prefer one over the other?

Heart wisdom indicates a deeper connection to the Universe. It is what we call intuition or the knowing of a truth without actual cause for the knowledge. (Principle of Trust and Principle of Connection) It is the cord to deeper intelligence.

When we desire clarity, authenticity and a higher truth, we ask the heart. When we want to know facts as they relate to the world, we ask the head. The head is limited to knowledge while the heart is tuned into our Higher Power.

Head knowledge is determined through your internal encoding, recollections and belief systems. When you live from your head, you are restricted by your past occurrences and mental boundaries.

Heart wisdom is boundless, never-ending, and unconstrained. Your heart speaks to you from possibility, opportunity and love. When you feel your heart energy, you feel vibrant, energetic, and guided to evolve and expand.

A Course in Miracles states, "But it is given to you to know the truth, and not to seek for it outside yourself." (page 617)

To connect with your heart, tune in to your emotions. Sit still in silence and listen to your body. Feel your body's flow or resistance. When your body feels lighter, you are in your truth. When it feels heavier, you are in a lie.

Trust and have faith in what you feel rather than what you think. When you are connected to your heart, you feel empowered and in alignment with all that is good.

—————— By Diane ——————

I've come to realize that the wisdom of my heart is the wisdom of God: the wisdom that bypasses my ego and the way I think things *should* be (given my limited experience) and helps me access what I truly desire — the highest and best for all concerned. The Principle of Unconditional Love (#4) helps me to check in with the wisdom of my loving heart when my ego is frantically trying to figure things out and is crying out for fairness or the need to "get it right."

Try these steps to access your heart's wisdom:

1. Invite Spirit in to help. We can get so tangled up in problem solving, we forget to ask for help.

2. Clear space in your mind to receive answers. Practicing meditation regularly helps to create space when we need it, to address circumstances that feel uncomfortable or scary. Another practice is to write down your issue and prayerfully hand it over to Spirit before bedtime. Ask for insights when you awake. The next day, try "stream of consciousness" writing to see what answers come to you.

3. Check in with your feelings as you consider your choices. There's a difference between feeling expansive/anticipatory/nervous and fearful/constricted/resentful.

4. Surrender the need to figure things out with your mind for a set period of time and leave it on the proverbial altar. Go forth with an open mind and open heart, trusting that answers are on their way, and then trust in the way circumstances unfold. (The most challenging step for me!) See if you can pull back into the role of an objective observer, releasing judgments and trusting in the form, content and timing of Spirit's answers.

5. Repeat as often as necessary until the answers you're looking for are clear.

By Sue

The heart's wisdom is based on unconditional love, Principle 4. Unfortunately, we as humans have confused and tangled things up a bit by adding condition after condition. When you hear yourself saying or thinking, "I love you but...," that is conditional love and doesn't come straight from the heart. It passes through emotions, stuck energy, beliefs we created or accepted, attitudes we adopted, values of the cultures we align with. Blend the conditions together and you have a big wad of gunk that the heart must traverse in order to express itself. Have you ever felt your heart getting stuck in your throat? That was probably unconditional love words trying to get past the gunk.

I grew up in a loving home. However, love was used to soften truth. I learned to totally dislike hearing the words "I love you" because the rest of that statement was probably going to be about something I needed to correct. "I love you but your room is a mess." "I love you but what you did was tacky." "I love you but you have broccoli in your teeth."

To access the wisdom of my heart, I must get past judgment and use Principles 5 and 6. In the present moment, I can open to possibilities. I listen for heart-centered words and intent. No, I cannot hear someone else's heart beating, but I am able to hear my own heartbeat. If I breathe into my heart and its rhythm, I find I can speak from that place and connect heart to heart with the other person. My throat gunk dissolves. Many times, I'm astonished by what I say and how I say it. Wisdom comes through me if I've opened the heart channel fully. I feel like the "FedEx of Heart-Centered Delivery," on time and complete. But not needing correction.

———— By You ————

1. What's the situation you'd like to change? (Just the facts, please!)

   _____

   _____

   _____

2. What opinions, thoughts, feelings do you have about the situation as it is now?

   a. Opinions:

   _____

   _____

   _____

   b. Thoughts:

   _____

   _____

   _____

   c. Feelings:

   _____

   _____

   _____

3. What results would you prefer? How would that make you feel?

   _____

   _____

   _____

4. How does this compare with other situations you've wanted to change in the past?

_____

_____

_____

5. What patterns do you notice about your own reactions, behaviors and results on this topic?

_____

_____

_____

6. What limiting underlying belief(s) do you have about yourself or others, leading to this recurring pattern in your life?

_____

_____

_____

If you can't identify any limiting beliefs, consider the following:

a. What opinion or judgment do you have about your situation?

_____

_____

_____

b. What do you keep telling yourself about your circumstances?

_____

_____

_____

c. When you think about your situation, what other pictures, persons, events or statements come to mind?

_____

_____

_____

7. What principle(s) would most support you in busting your old pattern?

_____

_____

_____

8. Are you willing to bust your pattern and experiment with a different approach in order to create new possibilities?

☐ Yes

☐ No

☐ Other

9. What bursts of inspiration have come to you about your situation after reading this section and answering these questions?

_____

_____

_____

10. What 1-3 steps are you willing to take now in order to create new possibilities? (Note: Focus only on what's in your control.)

_____

_____

_____

40

4

I've done so much spiritual work, why do I still have so many physical problems/ challenges?

ANSWERS:

—————— By Sherry ——————

This is a question I still need to understand.

Being spiritual or wise does not mean I have all the answers. What being spiritual or wise means is that I am willing to search and listen for the answers.

One answer that comes to me about why I still have so many physical challenges is that my experience with chronic pain was the avenue for my spirituality. The chronic pain caused me to search for answers and through my search I discovered The 7 Wisdom Principles in the form of the following:

- A loving, kind God.
- The ability to forgive and to be forgiven.
- Humility.
- Happiness and joy.
- The release of anger.
- A better relationship with my mother and father.
- The feeling of worthiness.
- An awareness that we are all worthy.
- A belief that I am enough.
- The feeling that I have always been loved and will always be loved.
- Faith in goodness.
- Belief in justice as love rather than vengeance.
- The understanding that judgment prevents us from love.
- The acknowledgement that God's will for us is always for our highest good.
- Our thoughts become what we experience.
- There is no opposite of God; therefore, there is no opposition to God. God is all there is.
- If God is good, then there is nothing else but good.
- We label the world through our perceptions and our perceptions are usually not of God.
- We are the creators of our lives.
- Our power lies in our connection to God.

I still do not know why I suffer from pain but I do know this: My physical pain is the source of my unrelenting quest to discover more about Source Energy. My physical pain reminds me I have much to learn.

I don't know the answer and I'm willing to learn.

—————— By Diane ——————

It's tempting to think of our spiritual work as a project with a beginning and end. And that once we're "done," everything will be fixed in the world of form — with our bodies, our finances, our careers, our relationships. I confess that I still have the tendency to look for progress in all areas of my life and when I give my time to spiritual practices, I'm tempted to look for something in return, the immediate relief of physical challenges being one of them.

The Principle of the Highest Good (#5) reminds us that we've been trained to evaluate our experiences as good/bad, right/wrong. Certainly, most of us would argue with God (and probably do) that physical challenges are bad. And we're tempted to offer our spiritual work in return for relief of our discomfort. But what if that's not the point of our spiritual work?

I recently heard a story of a mother and her young son, who suffered greatly from a debilitating disease, going on a healing, spiritual retreat. A minister on the retreat asked the Yogi master why he chose not to heal the son when he had healed others in similar circumstances. His reply was that he "would never interfere" with the contract the son had made with his mom before he was born. Her spiritual lesson was to learn compassion and her son agreed to help her do that.

We will most likely never be able to see across all dimensions of time and space, so we'll never know what anything is for at the time we're experiencing it. What we *can* do is partner up with Spirit to help us stay open to what we're here to learn and be willing to make peace with our pain instead of continuing to resist it. As we release our resistance, our suffering can diminish, and healing can occur that *will* lead to our greatest good.

———— By Sue ————

Maybe your physical problem IS your spiritual work.

We say we are born with no instruction book. Perhaps our bodies are our instruction books. Using Principle 7, Perception, "What we experience is what we believe," we can see that our beliefs drive our actions. When we have physical difficulties, perhaps it's simply that our bodies are demonstrating our beliefs so we can decide whether to change or ignore our thinking.

Some theories tie certain emotions to specific parts of the body. For now, let's take a more general approach and say emotions are stored in the body and are a result of our beliefs.

If you have been doing spiritual work, you are aware of the mind/body/spirit connection you have. Maybe all that work simply has made you more able to pay attention to your beliefs in order to examine them. What's been the point of your spiritual work, anyway? Mine seems focused on clearing out beliefs that no longer serve me. Do you have a different purpose? Write yours down. Now, write down what physical issues you have. What is your body telling you?

Next time you are aware of a physical problem, acknowledge the problem. Speak to it. Thank it for bringing a belief to your attention. See if it will tell you what it's trying to share with you. Stay in gratitude. It can be hard to thank problems and pain when they are active. Give it a try anyway.

Apply Principle 4, the Principle of Unconditional Love, "All love given returns." Love conquers all. Release the struggle and battle with your physical problem. Try nurturing instead. Remember that it's a messenger. Encourage the messenger to deliver the message. Once the message has been received, the messenger has no reason to stay.

─────── By You ───────

1. What's the situation you'd like to change? (Just the facts, please!)

    _____

    _____

    _____

2. What opinions, thoughts, feelings do you have about the situation as it is now?

    a. Opinions:

        _____

        _____

        _____

b. Thoughts:

_____

_____

_____

c. Feelings:

_____

_____

_____

3. What results would you prefer? How would that make you feel?

_____

_____

_____

4. How does this compare with other situations you've wanted to change in the past?

_____

_____

_____

5. What patterns do you notice about your own reactions, behaviors and results on this topic?

_____

_____

_____

6. What limiting underlying belief(s) do you have about yourself or others, leading to this recurring pattern in your life?

   _____

   _____

   _____

   If you can't identify any limiting beliefs, consider the following:

   a. What opinion or judgment do you have about your situation?

      _____

      _____

      _____

   b. What do you keep telling yourself about your circumstances?

      _____

      _____

      _____

   c. When you think about your situation, what other pictures, persons, events or statements come to mind?

      _____

      _____

      _____

7. What principle(s) would most support you in busting your old pattern?

   _____

   _____

   _____

8. Are you willing to bust your pattern and experiment with a different approach in order to create new possibilities?

   ☐ Yes
   ☐ No
   ☐ Other

9. What bursts of inspiration have come to you about your situation after reading this section and answering these questions?

   _____

   _____

   _____

10. What 1-3 steps are you willing to take now in order to create new possibilities? (Note: Focus only on what's in your control.)

    _____

    _____

    _____

5

How do I let go of my anxiety and/or depression?

ANSWERS.

———————— By Sherry ————————

If you asked me this question when I was in my twenties, my answer would have been, "Drink 3 shots of tequila and follow with a beer." Alcohol was my answer to everything back then.

My problem was that when the alcohol wore off, my mind still teetered on unworthiness.

At the root of anxiety and depression is the belief of unworthiness.

We don't believe in a better outcome because we can't see past who we think we are. We are worried about the future and consumed with the past. We can't live in the present, (Principle of Now) because our egos paste pictures of how life was wrong or how it is going to be wrong. Hopelessness ensues.

The answer is in our minds. When we address the cause, which is our minds, then the effects will change. (Principle of Focus)

When you become persistent in your thought awareness, you have the power to change your thoughts. Your thoughts drive your emotions and your emotions prevent you from taking positive action.

When you are in depression or high anxiety, your thoughts are not in alignment with God.

In order to shift your emotions, become acutely aware of them. Listen to your thoughts. When a negative or unwanted thought arises, instead of pushing the thought away, allow the thought to travel through you.

What you resist persists so the act of allowing moves the thought quicker. Then say, "I uncreate, destroy and cancel all emotions, perceptions, judgments and beliefs associated with this thought. I am an infinite being and a creator. I chose to align myself with love, Source Energy and gratitude. I release this thought to the Holy Spirit." (Principles of Focus, Now, and Perception)

Repeat as often as necessary until your negative thoughts are no longer controlling you.

—————— By Diane ——————

Growing up in a family of 10, I experienced a lot of love but also a lot of fear around finances. My 5th grade teacher told me I should "lighten up and throw a spitball," and I remember thinking, "how the heck can I relax and throw a spitball when we could be thrown out on the streets?"

Of course that never really happened; I was just AFRAID it would happen. It's our FEAR — "**F**alse **E**vidence **A**ppearing **R**eal" — that disturbs our peace whether it shows up as anxiety, depression or anger. The form doesn't matter since the source of our suffering is the same. It's what we're thinking that's causing us to feel the way we do according to The Principle of Focus (#2).

There are many methods to help surface the negative thinking that needs to shift. Here's a way that has worked for me:

1. Write down the way you would prefer things to be in an area of your life, e.g.: "I am healthy and whole."

2. Write down your own "argument" with that affirmation.

3. Hand all your negative thoughts over to Spirit for healing. You don't have to figure this out on your own.

4. Start looking for what makes you feel even *incrementally* better right now — a passion, a pet or a plant. It's not about denying what's making you feel anxious or depressed; it's about denying the "power" it has over your well being. It's about proving to yourself that YOU have the power to think about something that makes you feel good, NOW!

5. Watch your feelings start to change as you let go of dwelling on the thoughts that are making you feel anxious or depressed. Be patient with yourself. Trust in the process. As you shift your thoughts, your feelings, your choices and your results will shift as well.

————————— **By Sue** —————————

Being depressed or being anxious are judgments about the past or the future. They are filters blocking us from Principle 3, the Principle of Now, "Our point of power is in the present moment." Yes, sometimes we choose these filters to simply get through a day. It's the habit of using the filters that may be the issue here, not the experiencing of depression or anxiety by itself.

I had a traumatic shock once that rocked my world. I didn't want to exert personal power. That seemed too hard and I convinced myself I was too inept to move forward. I stayed stuck there for years. I limited my happy emotions, falsely figuring if I didn't get too happy, I conversely wouldn't get too sad. Or, if I didn't take too many chances, I wouldn't fail too miserably. I was trying to control the Universe when all I could control was me.

I explored several solutions. I found a shaman specializing in soul retrieval. I learned that in times of great difficulty, parts of ourselves may choose to disconnect from us. I became aware that we have many shocks and traumas throughout our lives. I thought I'd had one big one when in truth I'd had several that threw me off balance, so when I needed to be fully present for myself, I couldn't be. Parts of me were missing.

I welcomed back the parts that had split off. I made a choice to "return" to the present. I studied NLP (neurolinguistic programming) to learn about "parts" and to learn to converse with them. I learned other techniques to help me stay present in the moment and to break the habits that kept me from my joy and blocked me from interactions with others. My newest journey? To transform worry into accepting the perfection of the experience as part of my spiritual journey. Now, *that's* a habit worth cultivating!

By You

1. What's the situation you'd like to change? (Just the facts, please!)

   _____

   _____

   _____

2. What opinions, thoughts, feelings do you have about the situation as it is now?

   a. Opinions:

   _____

   _____

   _____

   b. Thoughts:

   _____

   _____

   _____

c. Feelings:

_____

_____

_____

3. What results would you prefer? How would that make you feel?

_____

_____

_____

4. How does this compare with other situations you've wanted to change in the past?

_____

_____

_____

5. What patterns do you notice about your own reactions, behaviors and results on this topic?

_____

_____

_____

6. What limiting underlying belief(s) do you have about yourself or others, leading to this recurring pattern in your life?

_____

_____

_____

If you can't identify any limiting beliefs, consider the following:

a. What opinion or judgment do you have about your situation?

_____

_____

_____

b. What do you keep telling yourself about your circumstances?

_____

_____ _____

_____

c. When you think about your situation, what other pictures, persons, events or statements come to mind?

_____

_____

_____

7. What principle(s) would most support you in busting your old pattern?

_____

_____

_____

8. Are you willing to bust your pattern and experiment with a different approach in order to create new possibilities?

☐ Yes

☐ No

☐ Other

9. What bursts of inspiration have come to you about your situation after reading this section and answering these questions?

    _____

    _____

    _____

10. What 1-3 steps are you willing to take now in order to create new possibilities? (Note: Focus only on what's in your control.)

    _____

    _____

    _____

6

How do we explain physical pain to ourselves?

ANSWERS

―――――――――― By Sherry ――――――――――

I am a survivor of chronic pain. Not many people use the term "survivor" with chronic pain. After all, chronic pain is not a death sentence… or is it? What most people don't know about chronic pain is that it kills the soul, steals hope and instills fear.

During my 5 years of intense physical pain and for the next six years of moderate pain, I was angry at God, myself and everybody who played a part in hurting me.

My ego was in charge and I was separated from love, joy and God.

At first I blamed God and then I blamed other people and finally myself. Why had I been subjected to constant pain?

As I searched for answers, I began to understand that physical pain is the result of the ego and the ego is our separation from God. (Principle of Connection) Guilt is the ally of the ego and the ego uses guilt as punishment.

Although we do not often confess to the love of guilt, we treasure guilt and use guilt to punish ourselves. We believe that guilt frees us but guilt traps us. It binds us to suffering.

A Course in Miracles states, "The world can give you only what you gave it, for being nothing but your own projection, it has no meaning apart from what you found in it and placed your faith in." (Principle of Focus)

The physical pain is my response to the subconscious belief I must suffer for the past. (Principle of Now) The answer is forgiveness and creating a new response to old thought patterns. (Principle of Unconditional Love)

If you change your thoughts and separate yourself from your ego, not God, you will change your outcome.

—————— By Diane ——————

On a spiritual level, we can explain our pain or other forms of disease with The Principle of Focus (#2): *Our thoughts create our reality,* and The Principle of Perception (#7): *What we experience is what we believe.* Our pain can wake us up to the limiting beliefs we're holding onto that we're bad, wrong, or not good enough on some level. Those false beliefs will create our reality in many ways in the world of "form," including throwing the body out of balance.

So, it stands to reason that if we can surface and surrender our false beliefs and replace them with the truth of our divine nature, our pain should go away, right? Well, maybe.

The Principle of the Highest Good (#5) states that everything we experience is part of our journey and can be used for our good. I can't prove it, but I've come to believe that we choose our circumstances in life in order to wake up to the truth stated in The Principle of Connection (#1): *We are one with all that is.* And it's possible that we chose to experience pain in order to heal in other areas of our lives.

The many physical challenges I've experienced are something I wouldn't wish on anybody. Looking back on them now, however, I can see that they forced me into many changes that I wouldn't have had the courage to initiate on my own, including "breaking the golden handcuffs" of my stressful corporate job, healing from addiction, relationship repair and ultimately, a more freeing, loving experience of life.

The Principle of Now (#3) can help us handle frightening, uncomfortable, painful circumstances. If we're willing to practice focusing on what we appreciate about the present moment instead of resisting what is, we unblock the healing flow of Source Energy and allow for more grace, peace and joy.

By Sue

You probably explain your pain as you explain everything else — from your filter of "The world is against me" or "I deserve to suffer" or "If only I'd had a different circumstance" or whatever your filter of choice might be. Maybe the only way you take proper care of your body is when it reminds you, through pain, that you must rest or feed it properly.

Principle 7, the Principle of Perception, tells us "What we experience is what we believe." I believe physical pain is trying to get my attention and is sending a message. I ask, "What are you telling me?" Perhaps it's something unfinished from one or more lifetimes, maybe it's something that belongs to someone else, maybe the pain is new to me in the present moment. No matter. I'd do the same process. Here's how it looks: If I have a pain in my stomach, for example, I go talk to it. I use neurolinguistic programming (NLP) techniques to manage the conversation. I acknowledge the presence of the pain. I ask its permission to speak with it. If it allows a conversation, I thank it for that. I find out how it's protecting me and loving me and doing what it thinks is best for me. I get its message, thank it again and then negotiate with it over leaving. It's generally ready to leave once it knows it can trust me to handle things from that point forward.

During this process, I might tap, using Emotional Freedom Techniques (EFT). I might use The Release Technique. I might imagine it removed from my body and sent to my body's highest intelligence, the Body Deva, for transmutation. I might visualize an open door and it leaves once an exit is provided.

There are many ways it can happily depart. I fill its void with unconditional love.

Consider changing your filters if they no longer serve you.

———————————— **By You** ————————————

1. What's the situation you'd like to change? (Just the facts, please!)

   _____

   _____

   _____

2. What opinions, thoughts, feelings do you have about the situation as it is now?

   a. Opinions:

   _____

   _____

   _____

   b. Thoughts:

   _____

   _____

   _____

   c. Feelings:

   _____

   _____

   _____

3. What results would you prefer? How would that make you feel?

_____

_____

_____

4. How does this compare with other situations you've wanted to change in the past?

_____

_____

_____

5. What patterns do you notice about your own reactions, behaviors and results on this topic?

_____

_____

_____

6. What limiting underlying belief(s) do you have about yourself or others, leading to this recurring pattern in your life?

_____

_____

_____

If you can't identify any limiting beliefs, consider the following:

a. What opinion or judgment do you have about your situation?

_____

_____

_____

b. What do you keep telling yourself about your circumstances?

_____

_____

_____

c. When you think about your situation, what other pictures, persons, events or statements come to mind?

_____

_____

_____

7. What principle(s) would most support you in busting your old pattern?

_____

_____

_____

8. Are you willing to bust your pattern and experiment with a different approach in order to create new possibilities?

☐ Yes
☐ No
☐ Other

9. What bursts of inspiration have come to you about your situation after reading this section and answering these questions?

_____

_____

_____

10. What 1-3 steps are you willing to take now in order to create new possibilities? (Note: Focus only on what's in your control.)

_____

_____

_____

WEALTH

Contents

7

How do I let go of being attached to the way I want things to be?

--------------- By Sherry ---------------

I ask for many things: a log house with a view of the mountains, a four-wheel drive truck, a booming business, a best-selling book, a sold-out house for my presentations, a thinner body, a healthy endocrine and immune system, and a partner who adores me. These dreams are what I think about every day when I'm not centered in my past.

I am attached to the outcome of these dreams.

So what happens when my business isn't booming or my book isn't on the bestseller list?

I wish I could tell you I float above my attachments to money, but I cannot. The choice, then, is to stay with the anger and frustration of not having what I want or to let go of the negative emotions.

In order to release the negativity, I look for the answers rather than sit in the problems. (Principle of Focus)

The answer is to align myself with thoughts of God.

A Course in Miracles states, "No spark of life was created without your glad consent, as you would have it be." (page 629)

If I created lack, then it was with my consent. I may not understand why or how I consented or what the lack of money represents, but I can determine how I choose to view my lack.

My choices are the same choices you can initiate:

1. Believe there is a greater cause for what is occurring. (Principle of the Highest Good)

2. Have faith that in what you created, you can also release. (Principle of Focus/Perception)

3. Understand it is your fear which holds you to your lack. (Principle of Focus)

4. Let go of the need to control in this time-space reality what you cannot control. (Principle of Trust)

5. Your attachment creates your suffering. When you choose to release your attachment to the outcome, you also release your tie to suffering. (Principle of the Highest Good)

────── By Diane ──────

The Principle of Now (#3) encourages us to remember that our point of power is in the present moment — not the future or the past, which don't exist. Since we don't know what anything is for, we can practice trusting that it is for our ultimate good (Principle #5) and relax and enjoy the journey as we go. Here's the process I use when I'm experiencing a situation I wish was different:

1. **I invoke Divine Grace:** I ask for help from my "spiritual posse:" God, Higher Self, Angels, ancestors, ascended masters — whatever you want to call them, and any name will do. I ask for help to be open to the spiritual learning that is encoded in the situation.

2. **I release my opinions and judgments about the way I think it "should" be or want it to be.** By holding onto my opinions that things should be other than the way they are, I am saying to God, "I can see this should not be this way. I have examined the evidence and based on everything in all directions of time and space (yes, I think I have that level of clarity, Ha!) I can 'see' it should be different." Instead I write down all the opinions and judgments at the forefront of my mind and then surrender them to Spirit, letting my spiritual posse do the heavy lifting!

3. **I forgive myself, others, and any circumstances contributing to my judgment of the situation.** As I forgive, I harness the learnings inherent in the situation.

4. **I cultivate gratitude for what I'm experiencing.** This doesn't mean I have to like what's going on, but I try to get to

neutral. I don't really "know" what the highest and best is for all concerned and I reflect on times when I or someone else said, "it was the best thing that ever happened to me," AFTER a lot of suffering about the way it was.

5. **I repeat the above process until I have a miraculous healing.** I have to be willing to trust the process even though it can feel excruciating at times… but I don't give up until the fear dissolves, and the answer is clear.

By Sue

First, I recognize what I am attached to. Second, using the Principle of Trust, "Focus on the 'what,' not the 'how,'" I check my expectations. I believe we are attached to our expectations.

Expectations can be tricky to find. Writing in stream of consciousness helps me to unearth deeply held, sometimes hidden, thoughts and insights. For example, let's take the expectation of how much money I think I ought to have or earn or be given. If my income meets the expectation I am attached to, fine. If I exceed or fall short, even if that expectation is hidden, I will feel uneasy. I might even think something or someone outside myself is to blame for my situation.

If my expectation — or attachment — is based on "how," I thank it for showing up and release it to be transformed into something else. It's unhappiness waiting to happen if I keep it. (I am sure to thank it for its service even though it doesn't seem "real." It needs acknowledgement to unbuckle itself from my core.) Expectations based on feelings can stay.

As long as I am living in an *expectation*, I am not living in the *present moment*. I am evaluating my present moment against the expectation I hold. I return to the present moment by either releasing or transmuting those expectations. First, I list all the expectations my conscious mind allows me to know. Second, I change all the expectations to feelings and not acquired things. If I want to feel secure, for example, that can come in many forms. If I am negotiating with the Universe that I will feel "secure" only when I live in a large house with an alligator-filled moat, that's a totally different situation. That's "how." If "secure" is "calm in my belly," that's "what." I do better with "what."

By You

1. What's the situation you'd like to change? (Just the facts, please!)

   _____

   _____

   _____

2. What opinions, thoughts, feelings do you have about the situation as it is now?

   a. Opinions:

   _____

   _____

   _____

    b. Thoughts:

_____

_____

_____

    c. Feelings:

_____

_____

_____

3. What results would you prefer? How would that make you feel?

_____

_____

_____

4. How does this compare with other situations you've wanted to change in the past?

_____

_____

_____

5. What patterns do you notice about your own reactions, behaviors and results on this topic?

_____

_____

_____

6. What limiting underlying belief(s) do you have about
   yourself or others, leading to this recurring pattern in
   your life?

   _____

   _____

   _____

   If you can't identify any limiting beliefs, consider the
   following:

   a. What opinion or judgment do you have about your
      situation?

      _____

      _____

      _____

   b. What do you keep telling yourself about your
      circumstances?

      _____

      _____

      _____

   c. When you think about your situation, what other
      pictures, persons, events or statements come to mind?

      _____

      _____

      _____

7. What principle(s) would most support you in busting your
   old pattern?

   _____

   _____

   _____

8. Are you willing to bust your pattern and experiment with a different approach in order to create new possibilities?

    ☐ Yes
    ☐ No
    ☐ Other

9. What bursts of inspiration have come to you about your situation after reading this section and answering these questions?

    _____

    _____

    _____

10. What 1-3 steps are you willing to take now in order to create new possibilities? (Note: Focus only on what's in your control.)

    _____

    _____

    _____

8

I can never seem to get ahead financially no matter what I do. Is there any hope for me?

ANSWERS:

—————— By Sherry ——————

I was born into a family where we heard the great triage of money fables on a daily basis:

1. Money is the root of all evil.

2. Money doesn't grow on trees.

3. Rich people are greedy and evil.

Besides being subjected to money fables, my brother, sister and I were exposed to parental squabbles about money. My father was a careful investor and my mother a squanderer. Together they created an environment where money equaled hostility.

Is it any wonder I grew up believing the best way to avoid anger was to avoid money?

Perhaps you stood in my shoes and found struggles surrounding financial abundance. Perhaps you equated money with evil, anger or greed. If you associated money with a negative outcome, you created the challenges you face today. (Principle of Focus)

Search your consciousness. Seek what roots you have planted with money. Change your thoughts to understand:

- Poverty does not equal happiness.
- Not all rich people are greedy.
- Most rich people are extremely charitable.
- God, Source Energy or the Universe wants you to live in abundance and happiness.
- What you lack in money is due to your belief in lack.

A Course in Miracles states, "All things are given you. God's trust in you is limitless. He knows his son. He gives without exception, holding nothing back that can contribute to your happiness." (pages 111-113)

If ALL things are given to you, what does that leave out? We are destined to be happy, joyful, peaceful and abundant. What separates our experience from what we desire is our belief system. (Principle of Trust)

Seek trust in who you really are and believe in your right to abundance, and then live that experience first in your mind and then in your reality.

—————————— By Diane ——————————

Of course there's hope for you! There's hope for us all, and it can be found in The Principle of Focus (#2): *Our thoughts create our reality.*

I would bet that everybody on the planet is experiencing something they would prefer to have otherwise, and the natural tendency is to try to move away from what we "don't want," whether it's a stressful financial situation, challenging relationship, or health issue. We put our thoughts and our efforts into trying to create a better future. But we CAN'T create a better time — sometime else. And if that's what we're trying to do, it will always escape us. The more we think "this isn't it," and insist on waiting to feel good until certain conditions are met, we will always be waiting, because our thoughts create our reality.

Instead of moving away from what you *don't* want, cultivate the willingness to create the present you want to have — NOW. The Principle of Now (#3) reminds us that our point of creative power is in the present moment. So we need to find a way to enjoy the path we're on instead of trying to get away from what feels so uncomfortable. And here's what's amazing: the more we're willing to do the work in our minds first, and choose thoughts that make us feel better *now*, the more open we'll be to the inspiration and guidance from Spirit about how to experience the prosperity that is our right and our inheritance.

This hasn't been easy, and frankly, requires daily practice. But when I am willing to consistently focus on what I appreciate moment to moment, things DO shift and change in a positive direction. I am better able to implement The Principle of Trust (#6) and keep my focus on what I want to *feel* — letting go of *how* I want to get there. It opens up the way for opportunities that are much better than the ones I am even able to imagine on my own!

By Sue

There is always hope. I must be willing to change something, though, in order for that hope to be anything more than a thought. I know I can shift hope to reality by making simple choices each day to ground my new life.

I've realized I can get trapped in the hope, though. I can expect every project to be "the one." But, I don't necessarily finish my projects. Who can buy what I'm offering when what I'm offering is unclear and/or not truly available?

Principle 2, the Principle of Focus, "Our thoughts create our reality," is at play here. I consider my thoughts to be like a mountain. Geology explains that layers upon layers of events (natural and man-made) pile on top of each other and forces interact and things happen and a mountain is formed. The mountain is a metaphor for my issue. If I wanted to move a mountain, I'd start at the bottom for the most impact. The same with my thoughts. I have beliefs and attitudes and values that run like a river under all I think. I start by listening to myself. I transmute my blocks and replace them with sign posts along my new path. Each transmutation takes a little of the support of that current mountain away. Each change moves me forward.

I thought simply clearing the beliefs, attitudes and values would allow me to get ahead financially. Nope. The clearing only got me closer by removing the blocks to finishing my projects. It's still up to me to take action. Knowing and releasing the blocks keeps me from asking, "What's the use? I'll never finish this anyway." I can confidently say to myself, "This is a different path. I am centered and grounded and am not being held back." That gives me courage and deepens and grounds the forward progress.

———— By You ————

1. What's the situation you'd like to change? (Just the facts, please!)

    _____

    _____

    _____

2. What opinions, thoughts, feelings do you have about the situation as it is now?

    a. Opinions:

    _____

    _____

    _____

b. Thoughts:

_____

_____

_____

c. Feelings:

_____

_____

_____

3. What results would you prefer? How would that make you feel?

_____

_____

_____

4. How does this compare with other situations you've wanted to change in the past?

_____

_____

_____

5. What patterns do you notice about your own reactions, behaviors and results on this topic?

_____

_____

_____

6. What limiting underlying belief(s) do you have about yourself or others, leading to this recurring pattern in your life?

    _____

    _____

    _____

    If you can't identify any limiting beliefs, consider the following:

    a. What opinion or judgment do you have about your situation?

        _____

        _____

        _____

    b. What do you keep telling yourself about your circumstances?

        _____

        _____

        _____

    c. When you think about your situation, what other pictures, persons, events or statements come to mind?

        _____

        _____

        _____

7. What principle(s) would most support you in busting your old pattern?

_____

_____

_____

8. Are you willing to bust your pattern and experiment with a different approach in order to create new possibilities?

   ☐ Yes

   ☐ No

   ☐ Other

9. What bursts of inspiration have come to you about your situation after reading this section and answering these questions?

_____

_____

_____

10. What 1-3 steps are you willing to take now in order to create new possibilities? (Note: Focus only on what's in your control.)

_____

_____

_____

9

How can I charge for my services as a spiritual/ energy healer when people expect me to do it for free?

—— By Sherry ——

I understand the belief that learning should be free. We have "free" public education and "free" church services. Behind those FREE words are taxes for the schools and the implied goody points behind tithing for the churches.

We get hooked on the word "Free" because we want to believe there are services and products we get if we are the lucky ones. And the truth is that we want something for nothing.

Research has indicated that when people receive money, a product or a service for nothing, they don't value it.

70% of lottery winners go broke after winning the lottery. It is also well known that if a product has a higher value placed on it, people are more likely to use the product.

While we want products, money or services for free, we don't value them when we receive them. (Principle of Perception)

Our responsibility to people as spiritual or energy healers is to provide them with the opportunity to grow. Since the human race is conditioned to equate FREE with not having to do any work, we must align ourselves with what people believe to be true.

If we gave away our knowledge without charging a fee, our services would not be perceived as worthy and people would be less likely to make an effort to do the work required to get healthy, wealthy or happy.

We must also honor and love ourselves. *A Course in Miracles* states, "To love yourself is to heal yourself, and you cannot perceive part of you as sick and achieve your goal."

We do not honor ourselves if we give ourselves away. We cannot heal others if we have no love for ourselves. (Principle of Unconditional Love)

———————— By Diane ————————

This question prompted me to ask another: why do people expect you to do it for free? If you're anything like me, it's because YOU don't value what you have to offer. It goes back to those limiting beliefs often buried so deeply we're not aware of how much they're impacting our thoughts, feelings and choices — choices resulting in reluctance to clearly state what we charge and honoring ourselves enough to stick to it.

Here's another question: what are you afraid will happen if you charge for your services? People will be outraged? Reject you? Abandon you? If anybody ends up reacting that way, it's about their issues, not yours. The Principle of Perception (#7) reminds us that the people and circumstances we attract into our lives are a reflection of our inner world. Take responsibility for your own fear and be willing to examine the "**F**alse **E**vidence **A**ppearing **R**eal." The evidence is some version of a false belief: "I'm not good enough, lovable enough, valuable enough." It's just not true.

Create a willingness affirmation to shift your false belief: "I'm willing to have a new loving experience of myself and the value I bring through my work." Set a price for your services that feels right and then raise it 25%. (Feels uncomfortable, but give it a shot!) If you have lots of "free clients," thank them for all the practice they provided and let them know you're officially open for business. If you must, offer a 10% finders fee for everyone they refer that becomes a paying client.

It takes courage and practice to think of yourself and your work as valuable, but you can do it. And remember, studies indicate the more we pay for something, the more we value it, practice it, learn from it and benefit from it. You owe it to your clients — you owe it to yourself!

————————— **By Sue** —————————

First, what do I think people are paying for? Second, how am I different from others who took the same training I did or who have the same "gift" I do? Third, what am I believing about history and what's "right"? Let's look at these in reverse:

Third: Many cultures have an exchange rate of some sort for spiritual leaders, the same as they do for physicians and other types of service providers.

Second: Each person, once experienced a bit, applies educational lessons differently based on his/her lifetime of understanding. I can consider my "gift" and see it the same way. I do not perform my work like anyone else. I took information and transformed it.

First: It's the transforming of the information and my perspective on experiences that my clients are paying for. And, I am an expert at my perspective. If I can show a person the way to joy, I can get paid for it. If I can lead someone through an experience so it takes them 3 months or 3 weeks to recover instead of the 3 years it took me, they owe me for the savings. Saving a person time or money is worth a payment. Set your fees based on the savings you offer. Think of your fees as being "experience-based" and "study-based," and not "spiritual-based." You took the time to learn what you know… and/or to accept the gift you have. Your clients are paying for what they cannot do for themselves.

Apply Principle 1, the Principle of Connection, "We are one with all that is." If we are one with all, then there's sharing to be done. This principle requires duality. I am trading one form of energy for another. I trade information and expertise for money, for example. And, I have worked and studied to get that information and expertise. It's a fair trade.

—————— By You ——————

1. What's the situation you'd like to change? (Just the facts, please!)

   _____

   _____

   _____

2. What opinions, thoughts, feelings do you have about the situation as it is now?

   a. Opinions:

      _____

      _____

      _____

   b. Thoughts:

      _____

      _____

      _____

   c. Feelings:

      _____

      _____

      _____

3. What results would you prefer? How would that make you feel?

_____

_____

_____

4. How does this compare with other situations you've wanted to change in the past?

_____

_____

_____

5. What patterns do you notice about your own reactions, behaviors and results on this topic?

_____

_____

_____

6. What limiting underlying belief(s) do you have about yourself or others, leading to this recurring pattern in your life?

_____

_____

_____

If you can't identify any limiting beliefs, consider the following:

a. What opinion or judgment do you have about your situation?

_____

_____

_____

b. What do you keep telling yourself about your circumstances?

_____

_____

_____

c. When you think about your situation, what other pictures, persons, events or statements come to mind?

_____

_____

_____

7. What principle(s) would most support you in busting your old pattern?

_____

_____

_____

8. Are you willing to bust your pattern and experiment with a different approach in order to create new possibilities?

☐ Yes

☐ No

☐ Other

9. What bursts of inspiration have come to you about your situation after reading this section and answering these questions?

_____

_____

_____

10. What 1-3 steps are you willing to take now in order to create new possibilities? (Note: Focus only on what's in your control.)

_____

_____

_____

10

How can I "Let go and let God" when I have to pay my bills?

———— By Sherry ————

The concept of letting go and letting God is a sticky one for me especially when the bills arrive in the mail. How am I supposed to let go of the need for electricity, a house and food?

This lesson presented itself to me when I departed collegiate coaching after 23 years without an exit strategy. I believed I would find success in a new field quickly and efficiently.

HA!

Perhaps the lesson of letting go is the one I needed to learn. Why else would I jump ship from a successful career?

Letting go is the act of faith when action has been applied. Letting God is the faith behind your actions.

The Principle of Trust explains how faith or "Letting God" become the focal point changes our lives. When we operate from the position of trust, we see ourselves as Source Energy. We operate from the idea we can have, do or be anything and that we live in an abundant universe.

What holds us back from taking action is our fear or ego which tells us we must be in absolute control, seeing the results before we embark on the journey. The idea we need to see how it will work before we move forward is resistance or fear, which is the opposite of God.

When we operate from love, peace and faith, we are Letting God. We use the power of Source Energy to move forward and work in conjunction with all that is calling those forces to assist us. (Principle of Connection)

Since God is within us and not outside of us, it is our charge to create our lives. We are creators and therefore we must do the work of creation while letting the power of love guide us. Our work is allowing God to operate within us.

By Diane

As a child of the 70's self-help movement, raised on a not-so-helpful interpretation of Christianity, I had no idea what this meant for a long time. And after health issues took our income to zero a few years ago, I would have gladly punched anyone in the nose who tried to soothe my fears with pacifying platitudes.

It took a lot of soul searching over the years and pleas for help from the heavenly realms (that I didn't trust even existed) to finally realize that it means this: LET GO of the *meaning* I'm making about my situation, which is just some version of fear, and LET IN the guidance and support that God has been lovingly sending me 24/7 from the moment I took a breath.

The Principle of Focus (#2) reminds us of the power of our thinking. We create what we think about all day long. Whatever "story" we have about the facts of our painful situations, if we're willing to take a look, we'll find underlying negative beliefs: some version of "I'm not worthy, not good enough, smart enough, lucky enough," some flavor of wrong thinking that's driving our experience. And it's almost impossible to create what we want in the world of form when we have beliefs blocking God's input.

This works for me:

1. I show up each day with a little bit of willingness.

2. I partner with Spirit: I ask for help to change my "story" about the upsetting situation at the root source. As I surface and surrender false beliefs — the *meaning* I'm putting to the facts of my life — I clear the space to receive my guidance.

3. I look out for the guidance for increasing my flow of abundance: an inspiring thought, a call from a friend or an article in a magazine. My "answers" are all around me. In the

meantime, I pay my bills the best way I know how, which may mean sending the smallest amount I can manage.

4. I trust the process.

By Sue

I've learned to surrender my situation to a Higher Power. Some people take "Let Go and Let God" to mean they have no responsibility after surrendering. I don't see it that way. I believe you are to "let go" of fret and worry. I am still expected to take action steps.

When I turn fret and worry over to God, I clear it from my energy field. When it isn't tripping up my thinking, I am open to guidance, new thought, and any number of solutions I might have been blocked from creating, or, more appropriately, co-creating.

I check to see that I didn't limit the Universe by putting conditions or limitations on my request/demand. I ask for what I want to feel, not how I want a tool (such as money) to appear.

Another trick is to make early requests. If, every month, I have trouble coming up with a specific payment, I make my request/demand of the Universe to be for ease in making that payment. And, I make that request early in the payment cycle. No need for fear and concern every month by waiting until the last minute to surrender and take action.

Principle 3, the Principle of Now, states that "Our point of power is in the present moment."

When I am in worry or stress, I am not fully functional. I don't think clearly. Part of my brain is dealing with repair or reorganization or regeneration or safety.

If I can reach a state of neutrality in the present moment when I am not judging or fretting or feeling consumed by emotions, I can be in charge of my destiny. My brain will be firing on all cylinders. I can see possibilities rather than limitations. I can transform a situation because in the present moment, if I am free of distracting emotions, anything can happen.

—— By You ——

1. What's the situation you'd like to change? (Just the facts, please!)

   _____

   _____

   _____

2. What opinions, thoughts, feelings do you have about the situation as it is now?

   a. Opinions:

   _____

   _____

   _____

   b. Thoughts:

   _____

   _____

   _____

c. Feelings:

_____

_____

_____

3. What results would you prefer? How would that make you feel?

_____

_____

_____

4. How does this compare with other situations you've wanted to change in the past?

_____

_____

_____

5. What patterns do you notice about your own reactions, behaviors and results on this topic?

_____

_____

_____

6. What limiting underlying belief(s) do you have about yourself or others, leading to this recurring pattern in your life?

_____

_____

_____

If you can't identify any limiting beliefs, consider the following:

a. What opinion or judgment do you have about your situation?

_____

_____

_____

b. What do you keep telling yourself about your circumstances?

_____

_____ _____

_____

c. When you think about your situation, what other pictures, persons, events or statements come to mind?

_____

_____

_____

7. What principle(s) would most support you in busting your old pattern?

_____

_____

_____

8. Are you willing to bust your pattern and experiment with a different approach in order to create new possibilities?

☐ Yes

☐ No

☐ Other

9. What bursts of inspiration have come to you about your situation after reading this section and answering these questions?

_____

_____

_____

10. What 1-3 steps are you willing to take now in order to create new possibilities? (Note: Focus only on what's in your control.)

_____

_____

_____

11

How do abundance and prosperity fit into the picture of being one with God?

ANSWERS

—————— By Sherry ——————

God is all there is. There is nothing that God is not. Therefore, how can we separate God from abundance and prosperity? (Principle of Connection)

"The Will of God is without limit, and all power and glory lie within it... It has no boundaries because its extension is unlimited, and it encompasses all things because it created all things… Because your Creator creates only like Himself, you are like Him." (*A Course in Miracles*, page 141)

Close your eyes and pretend you are fully prosperous. What did you feel? Did you feel light, happy, joyful, and peaceful?

These qualities are the definition of God.

God is limitless and abundant and if we are one with God, then we, too, should feel the power of being limitless and abundant.

In the book, *It is OK to be Spiritual AND Wealthy*, Deborah Atianne Wilson wrote, "Creating financial freedom allows you to have more choices and serve more people. This is your Spiritual AND Wealthy Invitation."

Can you serve more people if you are abundant or if you suffer in lack? From what perspective will you offer more to your neighbor?

By having more, you are able to give others more. This is true from the financial perspective as well as the spiritual perspective.

To discover the oneness that allows you to feel limitless, change your perspective.

1. God wants you to be in alignment with all that is good. (Principle of Good)

2. It is your divine right to be a creator. (Principle of Focus)

3. Living in abundance is living with God. (Principle of Trust)

4. Giving and receiving are the same. (Principle of Unconditional Love)

5. To suffer lack is the opposite of who God is. (Principle of Connection)

When you change your perspective, you align yourself with God and all there is.

─────────────── **By Diane** ───────────────

I'm tempted to reply, "How can abundance and prosperity NOT fit into the concept of being one with God?" And yet, I understand its origins and have experienced my own version of a poverty mentality: a belief that it's wrong to enjoy financial wealth or that we're not worthy of a prosperous life — abundant in health, wealth and relationships. The Puritans didn't do us any favors espousing false beliefs such as "money is the root of all evil." In my childhood home, I often heard, "People are more important than things," and I agree. But I can do a lot more to help *with* money than *without* money.

The Principle of Connection (#1) claims we're one with God, which *includes* prosperity and abundance. We can look to nature as a great teacher of this principle: "Consider the lilies of the field, they toil not, neither do they spin, yet... Solomon in all his glory was not arrayed as one of these." The trees do not lack for leaves, nor do the flowers fail to bloom. Are we not as important as they? (*Bible*, Matthew 6:29)

Too often we want the evidence of prosperity first in the world of form. Then we'll consider believing that abundance is our right. But isn't it interesting that the #1 fear of multi-millionaires is losing their money? Financial abundance doesn't equate to an abundance of peace and joy. It works the other way around: its substance will manifest in our experience as we believe. Nothing but lack of faith can keep our good from us.

If we're willing to surface our false beliefs about abundance and hand them over to Spirit for healing at the root source, we'll clear the blocks to our affluence — our flow of energy, peace, joy, love, prosperity. We'll come to expect and accept all that we need to make life happy and worthwhile.

——— By Sue ———

Principle 1, the Principle of Connection, "We are one with all that is," is on display here.

If we are one with all, and therefore one with God and universal principles and galactic laws and whatever else there is, and if there is abundance in the world, we are one with it. The same with prosperity. Doesn't that pretty well sum things up?

Before you start beating yourself up for not being prosperous or abundant — or for feeling smug and self-satisfied that you are more prosperous and abundant than the next person and therefore somehow "better" — let's just consider that we all have abundance and prosperity, perhaps in different ways. I know I have an abundance of extra weight and extra clutter. Looked at through that lens, I'm extremely prosperous! And, therefore, I'm one with God. You may have an abundance of money. You, too, are one with God.

Where's your prosperity? Where's your abundance? Consider that we are ALL prosperous and abundant. Does that help you see people differently? Does it help you see yourself differently? If you can see that you have abundance and it perhaps simply isn't in the place or way you want it, shift it. Come from the place of knowing how well you can manifest and start manifesting a move. For example, I might want to go from clutter in boxes to having my savings account cluttered with money. Same principle, different outcome. To make a shift, I'd tell the Universe I'm making a choice and making a change. I'd start demonstrating my shift by putting some amount of money into my savings account regularly. It's not important that it is a small amount. The Universe sees a shift and supports me. I can watch as that amount increases and I can feel the joy of abundant change in motion.

By You

1. What's the situation you'd like to change? (Just the facts, please!)

_____

_____

_____

2. What opinions, thoughts, feelings do you have about the situation as it is now?

   a. Opinions:

_____

_____

_____

b. Thoughts:

_____

_____

_____

c. Feelings:

_____

_____

_____

3. What results would you prefer? How would that make you feel?

_____

_____

_____

4. How does this compare with other situations you've wanted to change in the past?

_____

_____

_____

5. What patterns do you notice about your own reactions, behaviors and results on this topic?

_____

_____

_____

6. What limiting underlying belief(s) do you have about yourself or others, leading to this recurring pattern in your life?

_____

_____

_____

If you can't identify any limiting beliefs, consider the following:

a. What opinion or judgment do you have about your situation?

_____

_____

_____

b. What do you keep telling yourself about your circumstances?

_____

_____

_____

c. When you think about your situation, what other pictures, persons, events or statements come to mind?

_____

_____

_____

7. What principle(s) would most support you in busting your old pattern?

   _____

   _____

   _____

8. Are you willing to bust your pattern and experiment with a different approach in order to create new possibilities?

   ☐ Yes

   ☐ No

   ☐ Other

9. What bursts of inspiration have come to you about your situation after reading this section and answering these questions?

   _____

   _____

   _____

10. What 1-3 steps are you willing to take now in order to create new possibilities? (Note: Focus only on what's in your control.)

    _____

    _____

    _____

RELATIONSHIPS

Contents

12

How do I align myself with someone with a different belief system?

——— By Sherry ———

Stephen Covey in the *7 Habits of Highly Effective People* wrote, "Seek first to understand and then to be understood."

The question is not how we align ourselves with somebody else's beliefs. The question is how do we align ourselves with understanding their beliefs and stand in the space of allowance without judgment. When we live in the Principle of Unconditional

Love, we accept and own who we are without judgment which allows us to accept others as they are.

Our alignment, then, comes from the realization that we don't have to be right. We can allow others to be who they are. We can value them, present empathy and allow them to hold their positions even if their perspectives are far different from what we believe.

A Course in Miracles explains, "Understand that you do not respond to anything directly but to your interpretation of it. Your interpretation thus becomes the justification for your response."

When you listen to somebody else, you may not even be able to understand their words, because you have not walked in their experiences. Their world, therefore, may not resemble your world at all.

Who can determine who is right when the comparisons that exist are from two different worlds?

How do you align yourself with others?

1. Let go of the idea that you know their experiences and interpretations of the world. (Principle of Perception)

2. Believe we are connected with all people because we came from the same source. (Principle of Connection)

3. Understand that nothing good comes from judgment. When we attack others, we attack ourselves. (Principle of Connection)

4. Learn to focus on loving yourself. Through loving yourself totally and completely, you have no need for judging others. (Principle of Unconditional Love)

—————————— **By Diane** ——————————

This is something I practice consistently, since I have several family members who see the world much differently than I do. I used to try to sell them on my viewpoint because I thought my way was better and would serve them, too. I've come to realize two things: a) My way isn't necessarily better, and b) There are a lot of things I can learn from them when I'm willing to be loving rather than "right."

What's most important is that I align with the beliefs that bring me joy. One of the definitions of *align* is "to bring into cooperation or agreement." The Principle of Connection (#1) reminds us that we're all one and our minds are joined, so when I'm thinking and acting in accordance with my joyful beliefs, I feel an inner "cooperation" with Source and others. My energy flows without meeting a lot of resistance, from myself or anybody else. I don't feel the need to convince anybody to see things the way I do and I've learned to not even *share* my beliefs unless I'm asked for my input or I've gotten permission. And then I limit my comments to my own experience and what works for me.

It's common to feel judgmental when we feel the constriction that comes from misalignment of beliefs with someone else. See if you can shift from judgment to curiosity which will enhance your own experience: "What can I learn from them?" "Why do I feel the need for them to see things my way?" "What's the harm in having different beliefs?" "What's the highest and best for all concerned in this situation?" "How do I stay aligned with my own Source and what works best for me?" "Who can I connect with that *is* in alignment?"

The more willing I am to be open and curious about someone else's beliefs, the more I recognize common core principles. We may be speaking different languages, but the message is the same.

—————————— By Sue ——————————

An additional part to this question is, "What is the other person thinking, feeling and wanting?"

There are so many kinds of belief systems! This question can be answered multiple times in multiple ways. It's the definition of the words in the question that must be clarified. What kind of "belief system"? Religious, political, economic, personal or something else?

If I want to "align" myself with a person, I trust that we are all human and I have conversations on a human level — what sorts of things they like, what experiences we share, etc. I definitely don't try to change a person's belief, unless that's what I've been hired to help them do. And, I can't change that person's belief by myself anyway. Only the person can change a belief. And, changing a "belief system" is even harder!

I know people who erroneously think they can "fix" someone by helping them "see the light" or change their beliefs. Nope. Each time you try to helpfully "fix," the person might hear, "You don't measure up to what I want." And, after many discussions, that person may choose to find a discussion partner elsewhere. There's no aligning in that situation.

Why is that belief system necessary to you, anyway? Aren't there other things to discuss? Align where you can and agree to disagree about beliefs without needing to evoke change.

Consider Principle 1, Connection, "We are one with all that is." Maybe a person has differences, but, all things considered, we are both one.

Add to that Principle 4, Unconditional Love, "All love given returns." Shower the person with unconditional love.

Mix in Principle 5, Highest Good, "Enjoying the journey." Limiting your life to only those who agree with you could be boring and unfulfilling.

That looks to me like a recipe for universal alignment!

──────── By You ────────

1. What's the situation you'd like to change? (Just the facts, please!)

   _____

   _____

   _____

2. What opinions, thoughts, feelings do you have about the situation as it is now?

   a. Opinions:

   _____

   _____

   _____

   b. Thoughts:

   _____

   _____

   _____

   c. Feelings:

   _____

   _____

   _____

3. What results would you prefer? How would that make you feel?

   _____

   _____

   _____

4. How does this compare with other situations you've wanted to change in the past?

   _____

   _____

   _____

5. What patterns do you notice about your own reactions, behaviors and results on this topic?

_____

_____

_____

6. What limiting underlying belief(s) do you have about yourself or others, leading to this recurring pattern in your life?

_____

_____

_____

If you can't identify any limiting beliefs, consider the following:

a. What opinion or judgment do you have about your situation?

_____

_____

_____

b. What do you keep telling yourself about your circumstances?

_____

_____

_____

c. When you think about your situation, what other pictures, persons, events or statements come to mind?

_____

_____

_____

7. What principle(s) would most support you in busting your old pattern?

_____

_____

_____

8. Are you willing to bust your pattern and experiment with a different approach in order to create new possibilities?

   ☐ Yes
   ☐ No
   ☐ Other

9. What bursts of inspiration have come to you about your situation after reading this section and answering these questions?

_____

_____

_____

10. What 1-3 steps are you willing to take now in order to create new possibilities? (Note: Focus only on what's in your control.)

_____

_____

_____

13

Why are some relationships so much harder than others?

——————— By Sherry ———————

If we are all one, how can some of the relationships we share with other people seem so difficult?

Is it the relationship with the other person that feels so difficult or is it the relationship you have with *you* when you are around the other person?

The relationship you find so challenging is the one you have chosen as a learning experience to guide you to the truth. What is the truth you are seeking? According to *A Course in Miracles* (page 312), "Under his teaching, every relationship becomes a lesson in love." (Principle of Unconditional Love)

Who are you trying to love? You might think you are trying to love the other person, yet this person reflects back to you the pieces of you which you have judged. The lesson, then, is to love yourself and in so doing, share your love with others.

It is your own judgment (Principle of Perception) which holds you to the story that the other person is creating the problems. "You have judged against yourself first, or you would never have imagined that you needed your brothers as they were not." (*A Course in Miracles*, page 313)

In order to move beyond the challenging relationship, ask these questions:

1. What experience do I want to come from this?
2. What piece of me am I judging that needs to be released?
3. What can I love about myself that I can also love in the other?

To truly love another, it is your love you are seeking. It is not forgiveness from the other person which will change your relationship; it is self forgiveness.

"Only what you have not given can be lacking in any situation." (*A Course in Miracles*, page 368)

——————— By Diane ———————

There's an easy answer to this question, though admittedly not easy to implement. Our "hard" relationships are simply triggering our healing opportunities so we can learn and grow. And there's no wonder that the phrase *growing pains* is prevalent in our culture. Growth takes us to unfamiliar places that aren't comfortable until we've settled into a new way of being.

I grew up in a household with a lot of love, but no effective model for resolving conflict. Alcohol was used to soothe anxieties but then fueled the discord. I believed it was better to keep my thoughts and feelings to myself, carefully choosing what to share to avoid conflict. Hardly an authentic way to live and often lonely. At times I've felt that no one really knows me and wouldn't love me if they did.

So who have I had a loving but sometimes challenging marriage to for 30 years? A man adamant about telling the truth, sharing his feelings and demanding the same of me. Aaaaggghhhh — I hate it sometimes. But I also want the intimacy inherent in loving and sharing all of who you are and giving somebody a chance to love you back. The Principle of Unconditional Love (#4): *All love given returns,* has helped me transcend my fears and develop enough trust to shift my beliefs… and as I write this, I realize I wouldn't want it any other way.

We love our "easy" relationships with shared values, styles and beliefs. But they are only half the recipe for expanding as spiritual beings. If we resist the relationships that trigger our growth, they WILL persist in some fashion: same lesson, different person. As we make peace with our own need to heal and grow, it's easier to accept the hard relationships and shift to curiosity about how they can help us lead a richer, fuller life.

—————————— **By Sue** ——————————

Expectations determine a lot about a relationship. If I have expectations of the other person — what that person will provide, what I am "supposed" to provide, and vice versa — much depends on the other person. I might never even tell the other person what I expect (especially if I am unclear myself) and therefore the other person can't possibly fulfill what I want. Or, I might be in the relationship before it's clear what the other person expects from me. And, once stated, I might choose not to meet that expectation. Hopefully, I can get that figured out before I'm in the midst of misunderstandings based on misunderstandings.

We are born into families full of expectations for us. And, we have expectations of that family — safety, love, security, etc. Maybe your expectations came from your family; perhaps you saw a picture and made judgments. Perhaps you were envious of a family in your neighborhood. These are all thought-forms and made up rules and ideas and beliefs. They aren't real. Having trouble with a relationship? Get clear on what you want from it and discuss it with the others involved. Getting the hidden expectations into the light… no matter how silly or difficult they are to mention… will surprise you.

Principle 2, Focus, "Our thoughts create our reality," says it all. If I think in expectations rather than in what's actually going on, I perceive everything from that viewpoint. So, if I am keeping a secret "balance sheet" in my head and the other person keeps getting deeper and deeper into the "debit" column, the relationship will be much harder than if I express my expectations and alter them based on the true situation. This may not be an easy conversation, but it's much easier than continuing to work off undisclosed expectations.

By You

1. What's the situation you'd like to change? (Just the facts, please!)

   _____

   _____

   _____

2. What opinions, thoughts, feelings do you have about the situation as it is now?

   a. Opinions:

   _____

   _____

   _____

   b. Thoughts:

   _____

   _____

   _____

   c. Feelings:

   _____

   _____

   _____

3. What results would you prefer? How would that make you feel?

   _____

   _____

   _____

4. How does this compare with other situations you've wanted to change in the past?

   _____

   _____

   _____

5. What patterns do you notice about your own reactions, behaviors and results on this topic?

   _____

   _____

   _____

6. What limiting underlying belief(s) do you have about yourself or others, leading to this recurring pattern in your life?

   _____

   _____

   _____

   If you can't identify any limiting beliefs, consider the following:

   a. What opinion or judgment do you have about your situation?

      _____

      _____

      _____

    b. What do you keep telling yourself about your circumstances?

_____

_____

_____

    c. When you think about your situation, what other pictures, persons, events or statements come to mind?

_____

_____

_____

7. What principle(s) would most support you in busting your old pattern?

_____

_____

_____

8. Are you willing to bust your pattern and experiment with a different approach in order to create new possibilities?

☐ Yes

☐ No

☐ Other

9. What bursts of inspiration have come to you about your situation after reading this section and answering these questions?

_____

_____

_____

10. What 1-3 steps are you willing to take now in order to create new possibilities? (Note: Focus only on what's in your control.)

_____

_____

_____

14

How do I help someone who is looking to me for answers?

ANSWERS:

———————— By Sherry ————————

When others look for answers in you, it is because they don't believe they possess the answers inside themselves. They suffer from emotional, mental or physical pain and cannot connect with their inner guides to shift their perspective.

Because we want to help, we often make the mistake of trying to provide solutions to their problems rather than guiding them to find their own solutions.

Stephen R. Covey in *The 7 Habits of Highly Effective People* suggests that we help people find their own solutions through reflective listening. Reflective listening is a method of hearing what other people say and then reframing their statements into a question. This type of listening allows people to hear their words and provides them space and time to move gently into awareness.

Our lack of awareness prevents us from finding the answers we seek. We cannot see what we don't know, which keeps us thinking from the same mind. Albert Einstein said, "We cannot solve a problem with the same mind that created it."

We want to move our mindset outside of suffering.

By remaining in other people's painful mindsets, we add energy to their pain. (Principle of Connection) Ernest Holmes said, "If you mentally see a sick man, he will remain mentally sick. We cannot heal successfully while we recognize sickness as a reality to the Spirit."

If we cannot provide the answers, what is our job?

1. To listen without judgment. (Principle of Unconditional Love)

2. To see only love. (Principle of Unconditional Love)

3. To offer perfection in our minds. (Principle of Focus)

4. To allow other people to take their own journey even if it is not the one we desire for them. (Principle of the Highest Good)

—————————— **By Diane** ——————————

This question can be answered in so many ways depending on who's asking, the kind of help they're looking for, and whether you have specialized knowledge to offer. I'm often asked for medical advice since I have a background in human health. I can get anxious giving advice to loved ones, but the steps below have really helped.

1. The Principle of Connection (#1) reminds us that we are one with all that is. We have everything we need to come up with our own answers, though we can help each other facilitate the process of tapping into Universal Energy. Remember to breathe through the process of "helping" and keep your own channels open.

2. Clarify *how* they want you to help: do they want specific advice based on your experience? Do they need to vent? Do they want you to help them with a decision making process? A common pitfall is to assume they want you to "fix it," when in fact, they may just want you to listen.

3. Remember The Principle of Trust (#6): *Focus on the "what," not the "how."* Help them to focus first on what they want and why it's important to them versus getting caught up in *how* they're going to get there.

4. Give advice if that's what they want but offer it from your own experience: what's worked for you. Ask questions if they need help in making a decision. One of my favorites is, "Who else can help?" Remember to Google it — together if possible — if more information is needed.

5. Help them implement The Principle of Unconditional Love (#4) if you notice they're being hard on themselves or others, since judgment and criticism are huge mental and emotional blocks to accessing an effective solution.

6. Release any responsibility for the outcome. It's their choice to do what they want with your advice or opinion and/or come up with their own answers to the questions you asked.

By Sue

When someone asks me for answers, I first ensure that's what the person really is asking for. The person might just need to be heard, so "I understand" (or something else noncommittal) is the only response really requested. Or the person might want approval or support, so "Yes, you are right," would be completely fine. It's hard for me to "not help" by simply listening rather than giving suggestions and advice, though, so I tend to launch into ideas before clearly asking what the person wants.

I'm generally wrong unless I ask.

Interestingly, I've found that my suggestions for others are generally what would work for me if I were in that situation. That's because my own "reality" (see Principle 2, Focus, "Our thoughts create our reality") is in my head. I wish I'd recorded all the advice I've given through the years and inserted it into a book for myself — "Instructions on Living Sue's Life and Only Sue's Life." But, no, I mistakenly thought I was using my life experience and applying that to the other person's life. It's hard for me to remember that even if we are all one (Principal 1, Connection), there's a lot of separation in the world.

One great way to give advice is to use a "case study" approach. Take the basics of a person's problem, change the names of the characters, present it back to the other person and ask what advice that person would give to each of the case study characters. That's the advice that will most nearly fit the person's needs. Their own advice for their own issue. It's amazing how smart we all are; sometimes we need help seeing it. (Getting a person to act on that advice is another topic for another day......)

──────────── By You ────────────

1. What's the situation you'd like to change? (Just the facts, please!)

   _____

   _____

   _____

2. What opinions, thoughts, feelings do you have about the situation as it is now?

   a. Opinions:

   _____

   _____

   _____

   b. Thoughts:

   _____

   _____

   _____

c. Feelings:

_____

_____

_____

3. What results would you prefer? How would that make you feel?

_____

_____

_____

4. How does this compare with other situations you've wanted to change in the past?

_____

_____

_____

5. What patterns do you notice about your own reactions, behaviors and results on this topic?

_____

_____

_____

6. What limiting underlying belief(s) do you have about yourself or others, leading to this recurring pattern in your life?

_____

_____

_____

If you can't identify any limiting beliefs, consider the following:

a. What opinion or judgment do you have about your situation?

    _____

    _____

    _____

b. What do you keep telling yourself about your circumstances?

    _____

    _____

    _____

c. When you think about your situation, what other pictures, persons, events or statements come to mind?

    _____

    _____

    _____

7. What principle(s) would most support you in busting your old pattern?

    _____

    _____

    _____

8. Are you willing to bust your pattern and experiment with a different approach in order to create new possibilities?

    ☐ Yes
    ☐ No
    ☐ Other

9. What bursts of inspiration have come to you about your situation after reading this section and answering these questions?

    _____

    _____

    _____

10. What 1-3 steps are you willing to take now in order to create new possibilities? (Note: Focus only on what's in your control.)

    _____

    _____

    _____

15

How do I figure out how to balance the process of giving and receiving?

ANSWERS:

— By Sherry —

Relationships are messy. They are fundamentally the messiest part of our lives, because in our partner we see the reflection of all that we are not staring back at us.

Relationships are compromise. They require both selfishness and selflessness. We learn to listen and speak, to give and receive, and to realign and readjust. When we resist the intertwined process of the yin and the yang, we find ourselves overwrought with a piece of ourselves we can't tolerate. We don't like the feel of being unbalanced.

When we stand in a relationship to only take or give, we deny an essential part of ourselves. What we deny ourselves, we deny another.

Many times the culprit in a relationship is guilt — guilt for not making ourselves happy, our partner satisfied, not sharing enough, or not being enough. Guilt drives us to wonder if we are giving too much or too little. Guilt makes us feel bad because we want more.

How do we stand in balance? We practice these Principles of Unconditional Love:

- We listen and respect our inner guidance.
- We reduce the guilt we place upon ourselves and upon our partner for not being perfect.
- We forgive and forgive again.
- We reach out and ask, "Am I taking too much? Am I giving too much?"
- We ask for honest conversations.
- We listen to our partners.
- We listen to our highest needs and convey our needs to our partners.
- We stop giving what is not ours to give.
- We allow our partners to be where they are on their journeys.

- We allow ourselves to be where we are.
- We love what is.

——————— By Diane ———————

As the second child in a large family, I grew up believing I had to take care of everybody else before I could take care of myself. That idea was amplified with a boatload of axioms prevalent in our culture, such as "it's better to give than receive." By the time I added my own fear of being selfish if I expressed my own needs, I had become a giving machine with no idea how to receive. I effectively stopped the process by giving away all I had without filling myself up again.

The Principle of Connection (#1) and The Principle of Unconditional Love (#4) help me balance the process. Since we're one with all that is and all love given returns, the cycle of giving and receiving becomes one and the same: we give the love we already have, receive it from others and fill our tank again so the process can continue.

So how do we give without feeling depleted? I'm learning to ask myself loving questions and tuning in to the answers before I make my choices. For example: "What do I really want in this situation? What do I have already that I want to give? How do I stay open to receiving what wants to come to me? What would make me feel comfortable? Happy? Loved? What's the highest and best for all concerned?"

I get much better answers to those questions than I do to fear driven questions such as, "What will others think? What should I do? What's expected of me?" If the answer feels constricted or cumbersome, chances are it's coming from the ego, motivated by fear. That's a cue to change my question. If the answer brings some relief and feels lighter, chances are it's coming from Spirit.

By Sue

I have been terrible at receiving. Somehow, I bought into the lie that it was better to give than to receive and it never even occurred to me that "balance" had anything to do with giving and receiving.

So, then, there came all this talk into the world about standing up for yourself and asking for what you wanted and actually receiving it! The programs on getting what I deserved didn't work for me and didn't even make sense. They would require me to be — in my judgment — amazingly selfish and I thought that by receiving all that I was promised, I'd be taking away from others. Secretly, I suppose I also believed that selfish people won't go to Heaven and I wanted to go there. Here's the truth — I was starting not at zero to become a star and to receive what I "deserved;" I was starting at about minus five million because of all the beliefs I had to transform. There was no balance, no mid-point between giving and receiving.

Finally, using Principle 1, Connection, "We are one with all that is," I learned that my "beliefs" didn't square up with the world as I could observe it. I started looking around. Nature provided loads of bounty. One seed's growth didn't necessarily mean another seed couldn't grow and flourish. I saw many ways that nature "gave" and "received" and no one was calling a plant "selfish." If we are all one with everything else, why not take my cues from nature? Nature is full of balance and of giving and receiving. The seasons of the year represent giving and receiving. Sometimes, the ground receives plantings and then the ground completes the cycle by giving crops of food and beauty. If nature can be balanced, I could understand that I could also be balanced.

—————————— By You ——————————

1. What's the situation you'd like to change? (Just the facts, please!)

   _____

   _____

   _____

2. What opinions, thoughts, feelings do you have about the situation as it is now?

   a. Opinions:

   _____

   _____

   _____

   b. Thoughts:

   _____

   _____

   _____

c. Feelings:

_____

_____

_____

3. What results would you prefer? How would that make you feel?

_____

_____

_____

4. How does this compare with other situations you've wanted to change in the past?

_____

_____

_____

5. What patterns do you notice about your own reactions, behaviors and results on this topic?

_____

_____

_____

6. What limiting underlying belief(s) do you have about yourself or others, leading to this recurring pattern in your life?

_____

_____

_____

If you can't identify any limiting beliefs, consider the following:

a. What opinion or judgment do you have about your situation?

_____

_____

_____

b. What do you keep telling yourself about your circumstances?

_____

_____

_____

c. When you think about your situation, what other pictures, persons, events or statements come to mind?

_____

_____

_____

7. What principle(s) would most support you in busting your old pattern?

_____

_____

_____

8. Are you willing to bust your pattern and experiment with a different approach in order to create new possibilities?

☐ Yes
☐ No
☐ Other

9. What bursts of inspiration have come to you about your situation after reading this section and answering these questions?

   _____

   _____

   _____

10. What 1-3 steps are you willing to take now in order to create new possibilities? (Note: Focus only on what's in your control.)

    _____

    _____

    _____

16

How do I support others in learning their spiritual lessons without enabling them?

ANSWERS

———————— By Sherry ————————

As I stood in front of my grandmother carefully listening to what she wanted, trying hard to get it right so she wouldn't get angry, it occurred to me that I was an enabler. Yes, I wanted her to be happy and I wanted to support and love her, but when did my love cross over to taking responsibility from her?

The truth is that I had probably been enabling my grandmother since I was a child of four or five.

I learned quickly as did my other siblings that Granny had a bad temper. We could avoid her nastiness if we washed the dishes, vacuumed the floor and breathed just right. We didn't know better; we were young and following our parents' example.

How could we know that our support was taking from Granny the responsibility of learning about her anger?

"Make no mistake about his maneuver; the ego always empathizes to weaken, and to weaken is always to attack." (*A Course in Miracles*, page 330)

When you stand in the position of taking from your spouse, lover or family member a lesson they should learn, you are, in essence, attacking them. You might think, as I did, that loving my grandmother was the right thing to do… and loving is.

When does love change to attack?

1. We join in the suffering. (Principle of Perception)

2. We adjust the essence of who we are to make another person happy. (Principle of Focus)

3. We forget our main responsibility is to love unconditionally which also means loving ourselves. (Principle of Unconditional Love)

4. We try to learn their lessons for them. (Principle of the Highest Good)

5. We avoid and shut down our intuition. (Principle of the Highest Good)

To love is to see other people in complete forgiveness but not to join in their pain or attack on themselves.

—————— By Diane ——————

This question is near and dear to my heart. My husband has a disability which often triggers me into enabling behaviors — trying to do "for" him what he is capable of doing for himself. By trying to do things for him, I'm sending a message that he doesn't have what it takes to succeed. The Principle of Connection (#1) helps me to shift from enabling to supporting by recognizing that he is one with all that is, and is whole and complete despite any appearances to the contrary. I used to try to get him to see things a different way — "my way" — which I obviously think is a better way. But the truth is, I don't know that my way is better for him and it's not my job to teach him his spiritual lessons. That's the job of God, Spirit, the Universe.

Now when he expresses emotions such as fear, doubt, or anger, I can listen and acknowledge how he feels, letting go of trying to fix anything so that *I* feel better. That's not being supportive. It's triggered by my own fear, which comes from the meaning I'm making of our situation. The Principle of Now (#3) helps me to stay focused on the present moment and what's within my power to change. The Principle of Focus (#2) reminds me that the key thing within my power to change is how I'm thinking. I can stay focused on what's wrong because of his disability, or what's possible in spite of it. The Principle of Connection (#1) reminds me that I can reconnect to Source and interrupt my patterns of fear. I take a deep breath and declare the truth, often out loud:

"I am that I am, I am one with all that is." Through meditation or journaling I can assess my fears and question their validity. As I clear my mind, I'm guided to actions that lift him up so he can recognize who he is and what he's capable of.

———— By Sue ————

Using Principle 1, Connection, "We are one with all that is," I ask first what I, personally, am needing support about. I wouldn't necessarily have booked that act to appear upon my life's stage if I didn't have something to learn from it.

Assume we bring people into our lives to be our mirrors. Since the only person we can really change or help is ourself, let's use the mirror concept to look at our own lives. Some people give up their lives for others and thus keep the other person from learning lessons. That's enabling if it's constant. There may be temporary times of aid and that's not the topic of this writing.

I was doing some caregiving and began to worry about over-doing the help. I got energy assistance from some professionals. I then focused on what needed to change in me and not what I needed to do for the other person. I was clear on what I could physically do for the other person as a step-by-step methodology was in place. I got energetically clear on what I could do for myself and for the situation. By changing me, I changed my approach and the other person changed as well. No, we didn't have all rainbows and lollipops after that, but I was at peace for what I could do and I was accepting of where the two of us needed to part ways, or come together, for our own spiritual good.

I had to keep in mind that it was not my job to try to control the outcome of a situation for someone else. My job was to properly stage-manage this production for my own best and highest good, Principle 5, Highest Good, "Enjoying the journey." I can tell by mirroring when this journey ends.

——————————— **By You** ———————————

1. What's the situation you'd like to change? (Just the facts, please!)

   _____

   _____

   _____

2. What opinions, thoughts, feelings do you have about the situation as it is now?

   a. Opinions:

      _____

      _____

      _____

   b. Thoughts:

      _____

      _____

      _____

   c. Feelings:

      _____

      _____

      _____

3. What results would you prefer? How would that make you feel?

_____

_____

_____

4. How does this compare with other situations you've wanted to change in the past?

_____

_____

_____

5. What patterns do you notice about your own reactions, behaviors and results on this topic?

_____

_____

_____

6. What limiting underlying belief(s) do you have about yourself or others, leading to this recurring pattern in your life?

_____

_____

_____

If you can't identify any limiting beliefs, consider the following:

a. What opinion or judgment do you have about your situation?

_____

_____

_____

b. What do you keep telling yourself about your circumstances?

_____

_____

_____

c. When you think about your situation, what other pictures, persons, events or statements come to mind?

_____

_____

_____

7. What principle(s) would most support you in busting your old pattern?

_____

_____

_____

8. Are you willing to bust your pattern and experiment with a different approach in order to create new possibilities?

☐ Yes

☐ No

☐ Other

9. What bursts of inspiration have come to you about your situation after reading this section and answering these questions?

_____

_____

_____

10. What 1-3 steps are you willing to take now in order to create new possibilities? (Note: Focus only on what's in your control.)

_____

_____

_____

EMOTIONS

Contents

17

How do I let go of the past?

—————— By Sherry ——————

How many times have you noticed your mind living in the past? Doesn't your mind love to dwell there?

When you rummage around in the past, are you thinking about the time at the toga party laughing with friends until your cheeks ached, or about the time in Mexico where you played tackle football in the pool? Are you dwelling in those fun-loving places?

If you are like me, you aren't. You are probing some spot in time where you were frustrated, angry, or sad. For the fiftieth time you rationalize, justify or place blame in the failed relationship with your partner.

Does rehashing your past failures serve you? Or is this habit of living in the past preventing you from having the future you desire?

Since living in the past doesn't serve you, how do you let it go?

1. You reach the awareness that you've already been forgiven. Forgiveness from God has already happened. You are the only one who is still holding onto the judgment. (Principle of Unconditional Love)

2. You have faith that everything that occurs to you is for your own highest good. (Principle of the Highest Good) The moment you judged the situation or person was perfect. It was divinely orchestrated for you and the other people involved. The negative label you placed on the event or people was a label you created. You have the power to change the label.

3. You understand your power is in the present moment. You choose the moments which change your life. (Principle of Now) Remind yourself that you have no power to change the past.

4. If you can't change the past, what can you do with it? Accept and love it. By accepting the past and loving it, you experience a different future. (Principle of Perception)

———————— # By Diane ————————

For many years, I was a poster child for self judgment. I thought I was taking responsibility for my mistakes but what I was really doing was giving myself an excuse to keep indulging in self medicating behaviors because I felt so guilty. The Principle of Now (#3) helped me to reclaim my power in the present moment and live from the questions, "What can I learn from my mistakes?" and "What are my choices now?"

We all have a past from the minute we're born. And you can't be a teen or an adult on this planet without experiencing hurt of some kind — from you or to you. But there's a difference between holding on to the past and learning from it. If our hands are full, we can't pick up anything else, and so it is with our minds. Holding on to regrets and recriminations clutters up our minds and prevents us from picking up anything new. Is that how we want to live?

The Principle of Unconditional Love (#4) helps me to accept myself and others without judgment or expectations. I need to practice the following steps on a regular basis!

1. Decide to let go and forgive. Technically, the past is gone so I'm holding onto an illusion with no substance. I'm not denying my behaviors or those of others; I'm denying their power over me.

2. Shift to curiosity: "Why am I holding on? How is it benefiting me?" It can be easier to fill my mind with "could have/ should have/would have's" than it is to move into an uncertain but limitless future.

3. Continue inquiry: "What meaning am I attaching to past events?" I lost my job — does that mean I'm not good enough? My lover left me — does that mean I'm not lovable? I try to question my assumptions and my "story" around the facts to see what's really true. I ask myself how I *know* it's true and who I would be if I decided it *wasn't* true.

4. I imagine a new vision for myself.

5. I partner up with Spirit to help me let go of "what's true" and let in "what's new."

By Sue

Principle 5, Highest Good, is about "Enjoying the journey." By believing that all that happens in my life is for my highest good should be enough to allow me to thank my past and let it go to open up space for more goodness to occur.

Of course that won't work, or so I tell myself. I love the stories! Looked at one way, my life is just one Country-Western song after another. As long as I love my past, even if it's a love/hate relationship, I can't let it go. As long as I believe I AM my past, I am not willing to let it go.

Taking the emotional charge off my past — through detachment or other ways — allows me to easily choose to remove my emotional ties to it. I can then keep the story without the emotion. I'll also remember to remove the electrical charge anyone is holding to my past and take back any part of me that is being held by others. "Clean up my area," as the saying goes.

I use my "Big 3" — ho'oponopono, EFT™ (Emotional Freedom Techniques™) or "tapping," and the Release Technique to help easily clear what's ready to go. I'm now even expanding to a "Big 4" by adding the Spontaneous Transformation Technique (STT).

One teensy problem with Principle 5 is that "good" judgment concept. It's "highest good," not "good" as in "the opposite of bad." "Highest good" is about experiences and learnings of my soul and not about my human interpretation of the moment. I let go of the judgment of "good" or "bad" on a memory. If I can't get a judgment to "neutral," I at least am not allowing sad lyrics to run my life. If I still can't do it? I ask myself this: "What if what happened were perfect?" I relax with that, let judgment go and enjoy the journey.

———————— By You ————————

1. What's the situation you'd like to change? (Just the facts, please!)

   _____

   _____

   _____

2. What opinions, thoughts, feelings do you have about the situation as it is now?

   a. Opinions:

   _____

   _____

   _____

b. Thoughts:

_____

_____

_____

c. Feelings:

_____

_____

_____

3. What results would you prefer? How would that make you feel?

_____

_____

_____

4. How does this compare with other situations you've wanted to change in the past?

_____

_____

_____

5. What patterns do you notice about your own reactions, behaviors and results on this topic?

_____

_____

_____

6. What limiting underlying belief(s) do you have about yourself or others, leading to this recurring pattern in your life?

_____

_____

_____

If you can't identify any limiting beliefs, consider the following:

a. What opinion or judgment do you have about your situation?

_____

_____

_____

b. What do you keep telling yourself about your circumstances?

_____

_____

_____

c. When you think about your situation, what other pictures, persons, events or statements come to mind?

_____

_____

_____

7. What principle(s) would most support you in busting your old pattern?

8. Are you willing to bust your pattern and experiment with a different approach in order to create new possibilities?

   ☐ Yes
   ☐ No
   ☐ Other

9. What bursts of inspiration have come to you about your situation after reading this section and answering these questions?

10. What 1-3 steps are you willing to take now in order to create new possibilities? (Note: Focus only on what's in your control.)

18

Why do bad things always happen to me?

ANSWERS

———————— By Sherry ————————

Why do bad things always happen to me?

This was my mantra for years because I believed in Murphy's Law: life wasn't fair and only lucky people got to live joyful lives. I had no idea that my beliefs affected my life or that what I saw was a direct reflection of what I thought. (Principle of Perception and Principle of Focus)

Because I believed that bad things came in threes I looked for them. I usually found what I looked for. I practiced for 20 years finding the negative in every day. I became an expert in negativity.

Most people called me a pessimist but I believed I was a realist. I thought I saw life as it was.

What I saw was my internal beliefs.

A Course in Miracles states, "Projection makes perception. The world you see is what you gave it, nothing more than that... It is the witness to your state of mind, the outside picture of an inward condition." (page 445)

Once I understood my internal views created my external world, I knew I needed to shift. What I didn't understand was how to shift the thoughts I had thought since birth.

Ernest Holmes, in *The Science of Mind,* states "Life-long habits of wrong thinking can be consciously and deliberately neutralized... Merely to abstain from wrong thinking is not enough; there must be active right thinking." (page 143)

How do you get to active right thinking?

1. Take responsibility for what you see in life.

2. Choose the feelings you want to experience.

3. Align yourself with positive people who inspire and believe in you.

4. Seek books that teach love, forgiveness and happiness.

5. Practice the art of forgiveness.

When you believe in good, good will find you. You don't have to search for it; you are it.

—————— By Diane ——————

One of the biggest challenges we have when something happens *to* us, is that at the time of the occurrence, we have only our limited viewpoint. If the outcome doesn't match what we've decided we want, we label it as "bad." But our opinion of what's good and bad is based on our past experience and what we anticipate for the future — two states that only exist in our minds.

The Principle of the Highest Good (#5) reminds us that we don't KNOW what's going to happen in the future, so we might as well enjoy ourselves now. In fact, there are countless stories of people claiming that seemingly disastrous events were "the best thing that ever happened to me." Try shifting to curiosity the next time something "bad" happens by asking, "What can I learn from this?" "What's possible?" "How could I turn this into something valuable?" Then keep your mind open for answers and guidance from Source. Trust and give it time to see how it plays out.

The Principle of Perception (#7) also helps when we feel that "fate" is against us. It's not fate — it's life mirroring the beliefs we've invested in over time. I had a fundamental, unconscious belief that I wasn't good enough to succeed. It led to my working hard to achieve and I manifested many outward signs of success. But then I got sick and lost it all. Examining the false beliefs that didn't serve me contributed to my healing and eventually led to a career as a coach that is far more satisfying than my corporate career. Now I believe what seemed to happen "to" me, happened "for" me.

It's not easy to trust these principles when you're feeling fearful, but all it takes is a little bit of willingness to remember The Principle of Connection (#1): *You are one with all that is* and have access to all the power in the Universe. Claim it — it's yours!

─────────── By Sue ───────────

I have a friend who is suffering greatly because she's helping someone else. That just seems "bad." It seems she should be rewarded instead of suffering. I know another person whose grown children have problems so severe she has the phone numbers of a rehab center and the police on her refrigerator. Why is this happening to her? She cared enough to have these children; why is she in such despair?

These are "bad" things because I have judged them to be "bad." Margery Cuyler wrote *That's Good! That's Bad!* which points up that future events sometimes change our present judgments of what's "bad" to being "good" and vice versa.

Using Principle 3, Now, "Our point of power is in the present moment," a situation can be labeled either good or bad and it will be. If I've judged it to be bad, it is. If I've judged it to be good or a "learning opportunity," it could be useful to my soul's overall development and that would be "good," even if it's "good" only in the long run. If I am suffering, I take a moment to celebrate how much this opportunity has helped me grow. That's not always easy, but it can change my perception and label.

If I can get to "neutral," a point between "good" and "bad," that's the best place to be. It is possible to get to peace, or neutral, in most situations once I remember I called them into my life for a reason. I don't go to blame and shame for pulling them in. I change the way I view what's going on. There's probably something to learn and a higher purpose is unfolding. Once I remember that, take my power in the present moment and master the lesson, I can move on.

— By You —

1. What's the situation you'd like to change? (Just the facts, please!)

   _____

   _____

   _____

2. What opinions, thoughts, feelings do you have about the situation as it is now?

   a. Opinions:

   _____

   _____

   _____

   b. Thoughts:

   _____

   _____

   _____

c. Feelings:

_____

_____

_____

3. What results would you prefer? How would that make you feel?

_____

_____

_____

4. How does this compare with other situations you've wanted to change in the past?

_____

_____

_____

5. What patterns do you notice about your own reactions, behaviors and results on this topic?

_____

_____

_____

6. What limiting underlying belief(s) do you have about yourself or others, leading to this recurring pattern in your life?

_____

_____

_____

If you can't identify any limiting beliefs, consider the following:

a. What opinion or judgment do you have about your situation?

_____

_____

_____

b. What do you keep telling yourself about your circumstances?

_____

_____ _____

_____

c. When you think about your situation, what other pictures, persons, events or statements come to mind?

_____

_____

_____

7. What principle(s) would most support you in busting your old pattern?

_____

_____

_____

8. Are you willing to bust your pattern and experiment with a different approach in order to create new possibilities?

☐ Yes
☐ No
☐ Other

9. What bursts of inspiration have come to you about your situation after reading this section and answering these questions?

   _____

   _____

   _____

10. What 1-3 steps are you willing to take now in order to create new possibilities? (Note: Focus only on what's in your control.)

    _____

    _____

    _____

19

How do I keep myself from being emotionally "hijacked"?

ANSWERS:

─────── By Sherry ───────

How many times have you thought you were in control only to be hijacked by your emotions?

Last week as I caught a late night flight back from a seminar where I taught leaders how to deal with challenging team members, I wanted quiet time to meditate, reflect and relax. As I took my seat, closed my eyes and inhaled and exhaled a deep breath, a group of raucous people boarded the plane.

They yelled across the aisle to one another, guffawed at jokes and snapped their fingers to get attention. In seconds, I forgot all the tactics taught in my seminar.

As my throat constricted, I became more and more irritated at those inconsiderate people. Who did they think they were to interrupt my time for silence and meditation?

Right before I opened my mouth to give them a piece of my mind, I remembered the lessons I taught just a few hours before getting onto the plane: We cannot manifest peace when we are not in alignment with it.

Here is how I shifted my emotional response and how you can shift yours:

- Notice when you experience any emotion which prevents you from feeling good. Feel the emotion. (Principle of Perception)

- Let the emotion pass through you rather than resist it. (Principle of Trust)

- The moment you feel a negative vibration, observe from a nonjudgmental perspective what triggers your reaction. (Principle of Unconditional Love)

- Take responsibility for your thoughts and reactions to those thoughts. (Principle of Focus)

- Decide how you want to feel. Do you want to feel good and therefore get closer to the things you desire or do you want to be right about your circumstances? (Principle of the Highest Good)

After realizing that peace comes from inside me and not outside me, I closed my eyes and meditated.

— By Diane —

I'm much less reactive to issues that used to put me on the pain train all the way to Margaritaville. It's taken intention, practice, and a willingness to trust in The Principle of the Highest Good (#5), but I can get through the process a lot faster than I did at first. And the rewards are immeasurable: healed relationships, win-win solutions, lower blood pressure!

Try these steps. Be assured, they get easier the more you're willing to practice!

1. **Take time out — the longer the better.** Ask yourself if you *really* need to address the issue immediately. If you do, breathe slowly and deeply to buy yourself time to think and lower your adrenaline levels. If you can, remove yourself from the problem until you calm down — take a walk, pet a cat, take a nap. Do whatever you need to do to "clear your lens" so you can assess the situation with love and compassion for yourself and others. ("HALT" — if you're **H**ungry, **A**ngry, **L**onely or **T**ired.)

2. **Identify your fears.** Ask yourself what you're needing and wanting that you're afraid you're not going to get. Then ask yourself what the other person is needing and wanting — to be loved, appreciated, safe, to be heard, to be right? (Remember that we all have similar needs!) Take responsibility for meeting your own needs instead of expecting someone else to meet them. Ask yourself

what meaning you're attaching to the situation that might not even be true.

3. **Ask for help from Source for the highest and best for all concerned.** There is always a solution that goes beyond our limited viewpoint. Ideas will come to you if you practice some trust in this process and are willing to clear your mental space by releasing your judgments and fears. Everything that happens "to" us is an opportunity to learn, to grow, to forgive. Make it your intention to take the high road and let Spirit help you figure it out. Don't go it alone!

—————————— By Sue ——————————

"Emotional hijacking." What a great phrase! It gives me a fun picture in my head although the circumstances can feel less than fun in my body. I picture little emotions — all smaller than the whole of me by the way, but stored in each of my cells — rising up in some sort of revolt and then, in a super-fast exchange, I hand over my power to these little warriors.

What *was* that?

Here's an example: If I am introduced to someone and am making small talk and say something that causes the other person to have that "What in the world is she talking about?" look on his/her face, I feel embarrassed. That's because I have stored in my body some sort of shame emotions that that person's look woke up. Now I have Grumpy Emotional Warriors! Not good. I can excuse myself or try to "fix" what was said, but I am learning an even better way of handling things: not having the shame emotions in my body in the first place. If they aren't there, they can't rise up. Not bad, eh?

I "release" their ability to rise up by giving them permission to go and creating the conditions so that can happen. After all, using Principle 2, Focus, "Our thoughts create our reality," I first realize these are only thoughts. Using Principle 3, Now, "Our point of power is in the present moment," I hand them a decree of freedom rather than all my power when that super-fast exchange occurs. Using Principle 4, Unconditional Love, "All love given returns," I love these emotions as I set them free and they send love as they leave. And, like any good innkeeper, I clean the area they left, using the glow of unconditional love as the replacement. That allows me to radiate love rather than embarrassment from the inside out.

─────────────── **By You** ───────────────

1. What's the situation you'd like to change? (Just the facts, please!)

   _____

   _____

   _____

2. What opinions, thoughts, feelings do you have about the situation as it is now?

   a. Opinions:

   _____

   _____

   _____

b. Thoughts:

_____

_____

_____

c. Feelings:

_____

_____

_____

3. What results would you prefer? How would that make you feel?

_____

_____

_____

4. How does this compare with other situations you've wanted to change in the past?

_____

_____

_____

5. What patterns do you notice about your own reactions, behaviors and results on this topic?

_____

_____

_____

6. What limiting underlying belief(s) do you have about yourself or others, leading to this recurring pattern in your life?

   _____

   _____

   _____

   If you can't identify any limiting beliefs, consider the following:

   a. What opinion or judgment do you have about your situation?

      _____ _____

      _____

      _____

   b. What do you keep telling yourself about your circumstances?

      _____

      _____

      _____

   c. When you think about your situation, what other pictures, persons, events or statements come to mind?

      _____

      _____

      _____

7. What principle(s) would most support you in busting your old pattern?

   _____

   _____

   _____

8. Are you willing to bust your pattern and experiment with a different approach in order to create new possibilities?

   ☐ Yes

   ☐ No

   ☐ Other

9. What bursts of inspiration have come to you about your situation after reading this section and answering these questions?

   _____

   _____

   _____

10. What 1-3 steps are you willing to take now in order to create new possibilities? (Note: Focus only on what's in your control.)

    _____

    _____

    _____

20

What do I do when I've been on a downward spiral for a long time?

ANSWERS:

———————By Sherry———————

The questions we least want to answer are the ones we most need to address.

I've been in a downward spiral for a month. For the past 20 years I've suffered on and off from chronic pain. There have been long stretches where the pain is almost nonexistent and then stretches where the pain comes in droves. For the past month, I've had a complication of health issues in conjunction with the chronic issues. I've developed nerve pain in my feet and was diagnosed with hypothyroidism.

Under my current health conditions, I fell into the trap of asking, "Why me?"

The "Why me?" question signals that I am out of the loop of faith. I am not operating within the realms of the Spirit. I am operating under the assumption the body is who I am.

I feel sorry for myself and can't stop the human side of me believing that my body is me. I forget I am a creator and forget that ALL things happen to me for the highest good. (Principle of the Highest Good)

I repeatedly ask the two questions which keep me logged into the downward spiral:

1. Why me?

2. How am I going to get healthy?

Both of these questions are representative of the belief God is punishing me and I can't do anything about it. These beliefs keep me stuck.

A Course in Miracles states all of your problems arise from the belief in your guilt and shame. The way to stop the suffering is through total forgiveness of self. (Principle of Unconditional Love)

For the past two weeks, I've worked on recognizing when guilt arises and letting the guilt go. The pain is still there but my mind and heart are better.

———————— **By Diane** ————————

I was on a downward spiral for over a decade, feeling as if I'd NEVER get things "right," until an amazing coach helped shift my critical, judgmental view of myself and my circumstances. She taught me to live from The Principle of the Highest Good (#5) and cultivate a willingness to see my experience from a different perspective — one that was surprisingly neutral. Not resigned or detached, simply curious. As long as I resisted my experience, it persisted. The only way to ease my resistance was to surface and surrender my judgments and opinions and hand them over to Spirit for healing.

At first, it seemed as if my opinions were so numerous it would take 10,000 years to bring them all up and out. They poured forth every day about everything: *It's been too long. It shouldn't be this way. I must be getting something wrong. I'll never get it right. It's too late. I'm getting too old. We're always going to be in conflict. I'm so sick of feeling this way…* Yadayadayadayada.

I KNEW that my resistance was getting in the way, and at first I was tremendously discouraged because I couldn't help feeling the way I did about my circumstances. I finally realized it was just another opinion I needed to surface and surrender — the opinion that I *shouldn't* feel the way I did — when in fact — that's just the way I felt and it didn't mean anything more than that.

I opened up to considering The Principle of Connection (#1). Everything I thought was happening "to" me, was happening "by" me and "for" me — for my growth and learning and for my highest good. Once I started to practice that principle,

I started to believe it. And that's when my life began to turn around.

It's a principle that I have to practice every day… but it's worth it!

By Sue

Interesting about "spirals." I had a toy once… a Spirograph. With this toy, you could create circles and arcs and lovely designs. You essentially used a revolving stencil. That meant that your spirals could either be controlled or could be wild and exciting. You used colored pencils to add variety. My spirals differed depending on my mood.

Additionally about spirals, I heard once that you and your "soul mate" might be on spirals. Some lives you were at the same points on your spirals and you connected, other lives you might be at different evolutionary spots and might not meet or might simply brush past each other.

I've also been presented with the idea of a spiral as a funnel channeling amazing information from Source Energy into you.

So, when this question about the downward spiral appeared, I thought of all these things. What if the downward spiral could be Spirographed into a new spiral? What if the spiral could be turned upside down? What if your spiral connected with another person's spiral? What if you were trying to tell Source Energy what to do instead of receiving its wisdom?

Using Principle 7, Perception, "What we experience is what we believe," I'd answer this question by saying, "Change my perspective." To do that, I would need to step outside of my own thoughts, feelings and emotions and get new ideas, new solutions. I would get the wackiest advice I could and thereby open my brain to possibilities. No, I don't have to *take* the wacky advice. I simply need to convince my brain that I am open to new ideas. I can tune into teleclasses on new subjects, meet new people, attend odd-ball lectures, take some dancing lessons. I'll acknowledge that my current path isn't working and that I am ready for a new one. The new one will appear.

By You

1. What's the situation you'd like to change? (Just the facts, please!)

_____

_____

_____

2. What opinions, thoughts, feelings do you have about the situation as it is now?

   a. Opinions:

   _____

   _____

   _____

   b. Thoughts:

   _____

   _____

   _____

c. Feelings:

_____

_____

_____

3. What results would you prefer? How would that make you feel?

_____

_____

_____

4. How does this compare with other situations you've wanted to change in the past?

_____

_____

_____

5. What patterns do you notice about your own reactions, behaviors and results on this topic?

_____

_____

_____

6. What limiting underlying belief(s) do you have about yourself or others, leading to this recurring pattern in your life?

_____

_____

_____

If you can't identify any limiting beliefs, consider the following:

a. What opinion or judgment do you have about your situation?

_____

_____

_____

b. What do you keep telling yourself about your circumstances?

_____

_____

_____

c. When you think about your situation, what other pictures, persons, events or statements come to mind?

_____

_____

_____

7. What principle(s) would most support you in busting your old pattern?

_____

_____

_____

8. Are you willing to bust your pattern and experiment with a different approach in order to create new possibilities?

☐ Yes

☐ No

☐ Other

9. What bursts of inspiration have come to you about your situation after reading this section and answering these questions?

_____

_____

_____

10. What 1-3 steps are you willing to take now in order to create new possibilities? (Note: Focus only on what's in your control.)

_____

_____

_____

21

How do I experience self-love?

ANSWERS:

─────── By Sherry ───────

We like to think we know what love means but maybe all we know is what love is NOT.

We've experienced what is not love: jealousy, anger, judgment, obsession, hatred, doubt, angst, anxiety, frustration, and comparison.

What is love then? Love is the unconditional surrender in the belief all is good and will always be good. (Principle of the Highest Good)

Love is without judgment or comparison, without fear or doubt, without want or need, without guilt or suffering. Love is pure and innocent, angelic, golden, and synonymous with God. (Principle of Unconditional Love)

How can we know this type of love within ourselves? How can we fall so much in love with ourselves that we see only our good?

In the *Bible*, Genesis 1:27, the words are written, "God created man in His own image, in the image of God He created him; male and female He created them."

In *A Course in Miracles*, the words are written, "Love is one. It has no separate parts and no degrees; no kinds nor levels, no divergences and no distinctions. It is like itself, unchanged throughout. It never alters with a person or a circumstance. It is the Heart of God, and also of His Son."

We are like God, indivisible, created without distinction. Therefore, in order to find self-love, we understand who we are, where we came from and who we were meant to be.

We keep ourselves connected to our origin, remembering always we are sinless. We are united with all that is good and all that is right. Whatever we do has already been forgiven. We have nothing to prove and nowhere to go beyond our journey to reconnect with our God-like selves.

By Diane

I grew up wondering what it meant to "love yourself." It seemed egotistical, selfish, snobby and just plain wrong. We were taught the Golden Rule — "Do unto others as you would do unto yourself" — but if I treated others the way I've treated myself most of my life, I'd be abandoned by family, divorced, and friendless.

The Principle of Connection (#1) states we're one with all that is, and The Principle of Unconditional Love (#4) states that all love given returns. Technically, when we love another — including a pet or a plant — we ARE loving ourselves, and the love WILL come back to us.

But how to let in the *feeling* of love for myself? I've found that my blocks to feeling self-love are the false beliefs of the ego, various versions of "I'm bad, wrong, unworthy of love," etc. The voice of the ego may come from another, or show up as a "should:" I should do or be something different to be lovable. Either way, it's not the truth of who I am.

My solution includes the following:

1. Partner up with Spirit: I pray for help (throughout the day) to make the most loving choices in every area of my life, for the highest and best outcome for all concerned.

2. I intend to surface and surrender false beliefs causing me to feel constricted or judgmental of myself or another. I often journal to surface them so I CAN surrender them.

3. I practice "willingness" affirmations, e.g., "I am willing to surrender the beliefs that no longer serve me and have a new loving experience of myself."

4. I repeat the above as long as I need to until I'm able to change the "story" I have about myself and identify with the truth of who I am.

5. I consciously look for what I love and appreciate about myself, trusting that what I look for, I will find!

——————— By Sue ———————

I'll answer this two ways because I am reading the question in two ways:

1. How does it feel when self-love is present?

   There are many ways I experience self-love. One is self-acceptance without judgment. Yes, I "should" be going for joy or higher emotions, but I'm happy just to have critical voices in my head be quiet. I am at peace.

   I have been very lucky in my life to have physically experienced being enfolded by angel's wings on two different occasions. I know the feeling of unconditional love and it's amazing. Once you experience unconditional love, it's more than a concept. It's a blanket to wrap yourself up in and snuggle with and enjoy. Principle 4, Unconditional Love: "All love given returns," is what I think self-love is. Yes, Principle 4 speaks to all love given being returned, so it's not totally what I am referencing. However, it seems impossible to keep that energy to yourself. It's bound to spill over onto others in your sphere. Being selfish with self-love just doesn't seem possible.

2. What, exactly, do I do in order to meet my own definition of self-love?

   As a way to experience self-love, I believe I, personally, spend time alone. Not needing or being needed. Or, I go somewhere by myself, like a concert in a park or a crowded subway. Again, not needing or being needed. But, here's the hook: once my heart is exceedingly full, it spills out in conversation with total strangers. We share time and exchange perspectives for brief moments and that heart to heart connection validates my self-love. It's enough to simply fill my heart. I don't need to receive validation or know of any effect I have on anyone. That's where the lack of judgment is so useful. At that moment, I'm loving who I am and that's plenty.

By You

1. What's the situation you'd like to change? (Just the facts, please!)

   _____

   _____

   _____

2. What opinions, thoughts, feelings do you have about the situation as it is now?

   a. Opinions:

   _____

   _____

   _____

   b. Thoughts:

   _____

   _____

   _____

c. Feelings:

_____

_____

_____

3. What results would you prefer? How would that make you feel?

_____

_____

_____

4. How does this compare with other situations you've wanted to change in the past?

_____

_____

_____

5. What patterns do you notice about your own reactions, behaviors and results on this topic?

_____

_____

_____

6. What limiting underlying belief(s) do you have about yourself or others, leading to this recurring pattern in your life?

_____

_____

_____

If you can't identify any limiting beliefs, consider the following:

a. What opinion or judgment do you have about your situation?

_____

_____

_____

b. What do you keep telling yourself about your circumstances?

_____

_____

_____

c. When you think about your situation, what other pictures, persons, events or statements come to mind?

_____

_____

_____

7. What principle(s) would most support you in busting your old pattern?

_____

_____

_____

8. Are you willing to bust your pattern and experiment with a different approach in order to create new possibilities?

☐ Yes

☐ No

☐ Other

9. What bursts of inspiration have come to you about your situation after reading this section and answering these questions?

_____

_____

_____

10. What 1-3 steps are you willing to take now in order to create new possibilities? (Note: Focus only on what's in your control.)

_____

_____

_____

About the Authors

If you have come to this section it's most likely for one of three reasons:

1. You have a penchant for "About the Author" pages and go from book to book marveling about who's crazy enough to put all this stuff out into the world.

2. You're obsessive about reading books from cover to cover whether you like what you're reading or not.

Or...

3. There was something that piqued your interest in what you read and you want to know more about who wrote it.

In the case of #3, we're guessing you have some additional questions. Some version of the five primary questions that aficionados of the "personal growth" genre often have floating around in their consciousness:

1. Do I like these authors?

2. Do I trust them?

3. Can they help me?

4. What would it be like to work with them?

5. How do I contact them?

On the following pages, we will do our best to answer those questions for you.

Thanks for asking!

Sherry, Diane and Sue

———— Coach Sherry M. Winn ————

Coach Sherry Winn is an in-demand motivational speaker, a leading success coach and seminar trainer, a two-time Olympian, a national championship basketball coach, and an Amazon best seller. She has written five books, including *Unleash the Winner Within You: A Success Game Plan for Business, Leadership and Life.* Thousands, from small business owners to athletic coaches to corporate executives, have enjoyed Coach Winn's powerful interactive and humorous WINNING presentations.

With over 34 years of practicing leadership as an elite athlete and collegiate basketball coach, Sherry is an expert on coaching leaders and team members to championship status. She has successfully taken people beyond their levels of comfort to "WIN" against competitors who were superior in talent, facilities and financial budgets. Through her WIN Philosophy™ and WINNER Principles™, she teaches leaders and team members to be victorious even when the odds appear to be insurmountable.

A recognized authority on leadership and team development, Coach Winn shares with you the WINNER Principles which will enable you to rejuvenate, invigorate and stimulate you and your team members to become agents of change.

Audiences rave about Coach Winn's ability to enthusiastically deliver messages woven into humorous stories which are applicable for individuals within all levels of organizations. A passionate, sought-after author, speaker and business consultant, Coach Winn is characterized by friends, colleagues and clients as one of the most benevolent, perceptive and influential individuals in the business today.

Coach Winn is the originator of the WIN Philosophy™ and the WINNER Principles™, and is known for her passion and belief system that ALL things are possible.

To book Coach Winn for a media appearance, speaking or seminar engagements, or to inquire about her WINNING Coaching, call 304-380-4398, email her at **coachwinn@coachwinnspeaks. com** or visit her website at **www.coachwinnspeaks.com**. You can follow Coach Winn at **www.facebook.com/coachwinnspeaks** or **www.twitter.com/coachwinnspeaks**.

Diane Chew

Diane is a life transition specialist whose passion is coaching women who want to recover their brilliance after experiencing challenges that have threatened to dull their inner light. If you're facing transitions by "design" such as retirement or the empty nest experience, or transitions by "default" due to divorce, career changes or health issues, Diane can help you to leverage those transitions as a springboard to higher levels of satisfaction with your health, wealth and relationships.

Diane has a natural affinity for personal development, training and coaching which she honed to an art to survive the stresses of a 30 year corporate career and led to her certification as a life and business coach. But it was her own experiences with a near fatal auto-immune disease, job loss, addiction, financial instability and the need to care for a disabled husband that inspired her to dive deeply into both scientific and spiritual approaches to emotional and physical healing.

Her certifications range from "Behavioral and Values Analyst" to "Advanced Emotional Freedom Techniques Practitioner," and she is an avid student of *A Course in Miracles*. She delights in exploring tools and techniques that appeal to the objective and subjective perspective, to the right and left brain, and to the scientist, the business person and the spiritualist. Her gift is to find the perfect blend for each client, offering a customized approach seldom found in a single coaching program.

Diane is a master at helping clients to better understand themselves and remove the blocks to the lives they desire. She serves as a gentle but firm guide — helping clients to develop their personalized success strategy so they can immediately experience life's pleasures NOW — even as they start to close the gap from where they are to where they want to be physically, mentally, emotionally and spiritually.

Diane is an Amazon Best Selling Author and the originator of the internationally popular coaching programs, *Change Your*

Story, Change Your Life and *The Art of Receiving: How to Get Just What You Want, Using Just What You Have.*

Diane is a firm believer that life can be filled with laughter and fun, no matter what circumstances you're facing. Her life hasn't been a cakewalk, but she's never lost her smile or her passion for helping others find joy in the journey.

Diane is committed to exploring the possibilities of working with potential clients through in depth discovery dialogues so that you can decide if it's "hell yes!" or "hell no!" To schedule your complimentary session, contact Diane directly at **dianechew@comcast.net** and put "schedule coaching conversation" in the subject line. You can also visit her website: **www.recoveryourbrilliance.com** or follow her on Facebook at **www.facebook.com/simplysuccessfulcoaching.**

Virginia Sue Tarlton

Sue Tarlton is a life/business/personal coach, energist, speaker, philosopher and visionary. She is a neurolinguistic programming master practitioner who consistently explores a wide range of interesting concepts that she incorporates in her coaching. She also is a certified tapping practitioner and Spontaneous Transformation Technique practitioner and uses those energy techniques to clear clients' blocks to a more satisfying life. Her individually-tailored coaching solutions have helped clients and audiences increase their personal effectiveness. Sue's current mission is to encourage tapping's acceptance in schools and organizations **(tappinginschools.com).**

Sue incorporates her previous experiences in the corporate world, in the small business and entrepreneurial world, in the for-profit and non-profit sectors, as well as in small towns and large cities in her writings, coaching and consulting. She has a wide range of first-hand experiences that have deepened her understanding of her clients and their needs. Her superior listening skills enable her to clarify seemingly large issues into smaller, manageable pieces so successful solutions can be determined and real progress accomplished.

Above all, Sue is creative. She designed products that were so odd she was encouraged to take up stand-up comedy as a better outlet than actual manufacturing. She also created an app for tapping that allows individuals to type in their own issues and solve them in a do-it-yourself manner (etapapp.com). Her blog at 2stopsue.com chronicles people she meets in her travels and the interesting and enlightening conversations they have. Her audio workbook, *Getting to Know You: Strategies for Effective (and Fun!) Conversations,* is available at 2stopsue.com.

Sue has created a set of journals for creating a business in a year. "Biz in a Year" journals are divided into chunks of weeks, with one journal available that covers all 52 weeks. Sue understands that some business processes take time to develop and this journal set allows a person to take a year or less to turn dreams into reality. Visit Amazon.com or Bizinayear.com for more information.

Additionally, Sue authored *Mother Tourista's Helping Hand(Book): Your New York City Companion* (now out of print), started an on-line store, created websites, developed international communities, conducted radio interviews, produced and narrated a television show and a radio show, and studies energy and spirituality. Her next projects will probably center around dignity. She's a lifelong learner and believes in teaching what she's found useful to her life. She also shares random, useless information as conversation starters and as a way to redirect monologues. She currently lives in New York City.

Want to creatively and successfully open up to the rest of your life? Contact Sue through **sue@tappinginschools.com**.

Acknowledgements

————————— From Sherry —————————

Thank you to the people who dared to become aware of their higher selves, who spent time in meditation, silence and reading to share their wisdom with me. I honor Dr. Wayne Dyer, Deepak Chopra, Ernest Holmes, Diane Chew, Sue Tarlton, and the many other spiritual people who have allowed me to hear my inner spirit. I also acknowledge Helen Schucman, the Scribe for *A Course in Miracles*.

————————— From Diane —————————

With great gratitude:

- For my "spiritual posse" and your unconditional love:
  my loyal, faithful and loving husband, Ben, my dear family,
  co-authors Sherry Winn and Sue Tarlton and my amazing
  coach, Candace Smolowe, who introduced me to *A Course
  in Miracles* and has continued to remind me that "the light
  has already come!"

- For the countless earth angels who have shared their wisdom so I didn't have to figure it all out by myself: Dr. Wayne Dyer, Louise Hay, Esther and Jerry Hicks, Bruce Lipton, Jennifer Hadley, Tara Brach, Julia Cameron, Sark, and many, many more.

- For all the readers who are showing up for their own lives and joining us on this journey of awakening to the truth of who we are and why we're here.

——————— From Sue ———————

Enormous thanks to the people who've provided life lessons and guidance to me. I thank my family and friends for their remarkable constancy, teachings and support. I am extraordinarily grateful to my co-authors, Diane Chew and Sherry Winn, for allowing me to join them in this exploration. Their inspired wisdom has been invaluable to me.

Special thanks to Niky Rey and Colette Stefan who have guided and strengthened me while sharing new perspectives and allowing me to reach new levels of understanding.

There are so many open-hearted people to thank who are guides and mentors without even knowing it! Oprah Winfrey, Dr. Ihaleakala Hew Len, Joe Vitale, Steven Leeds, Rachel Hott, Trudy Raschkind Steinfeld, Margaret Lynch, Donna Eden, Gary Craig, CJ Puotinen, Jennifer McLean, Eram Saeed, Larry Crane, plus the strangers who've shared their stories and opened my appreciation for the magnificence of the human spirit. I am glad to know we are all one.